meet me in my mind

by Natasha Chinoy
//Rainbow//

Published by Zana Books

Zana Books
Visit ZanaBooks.com
Printed in Canada
ISBN # 9 780988 164796

Cover Design: Lenka Cita
Sketch artist: Freddie Mama

RAINBOW POT

I simply want to help the ones I can while keeping my life simple.

So here is the deal my dear friends and strangers.

Grab a book, touch it, feel it, read it and live it. Or use it as a doorstop if you don't connect to it.

Feel free to dig deep into your pocket and between the pillows of your couch, grab some dollar bills and donate it to what I call the Rainbow Pot.

I will donate all the money from the Rainbow Pot to a cause I feel connected to.

What will be the cause? I have no idea? It might be a family in need of groceries; it might be a child in the hospital wanting a special gift...

More questions?

Well I probably don't have the answer.

I simply just want:

- Teenagers to feel like they are not alone when they read this book.
- Parents to open their eyes and ears and understand us.

And in this amazing process of growing together, I want to be able to help those that cross my path with the money from the Rainbow Pot.

Natasha Chinoy :)

Table of contents

DEDICATION

Why Rainbow?

I used to talk to this old woman in a nursing home where I volunteered. Her name was June Collins. Whenever I came in, all her clothes were full of rainbows. She even had rainbow everything: her clothes, her shoes, her jewelry, her blankets, her pillows, even her emergency button (in case she fell down). Everything of hers was full of rainbows. So one day I asked her:

"June, why do you have sooo many rainbows everywhere I look?"

She told me to come near her bed and whispered in my ear.

"Have you ever looked at a rainbow without smiling?"

When I thought about it, I said:

"No, actually no."

Then she said:

"A rainbow is a symbol of love and happiness. In your life you will come across horrible things and horrible people. But as long as you see the colors of the rainbow, you will never be sad. So whenever people think of me, they will smile. Also, why the hell not?"

She made me laugh every time I came to the nursing home. She was so full of life! I knew her for two years. Unfortunately, after she talked to me about the rainbow, she passed away three days later. When I found out, I cried for several hours. The next day I came into the nursing home and I found a box with my name on it in June's room. In it were half the things she owned that were covered in rainbows and a note that said:

"Thank you for these last two years. It was a pleasure to get to know you. Please take these things and know that whenever you see a rainbow, I'll be there to see you smile."

I have never told anyone about this before. She touched my heart, and that is the true reason why I need the Rainbow name to carry on. You see, Rainbow is a real person. She is June.

I AM MY FAMILY

Mom (*Kashmira*): A caregiver with a heart of gold. She dazzles me and also sometimes annoys me with how intelligent she is. As I describe her intense intellect, an alien from another planet. But she is my alien and I love her with my whole heart even though I know I do not express it enough.

Dad (*Zubin*): My Dad is the one who taught me the value of interacting with people. He is the most likable person I know. Everyone we meet is obsessed with him and I have to say, so am I. I'm proud of him and all his accomplishments in life.

Brother (*Zal*): Oh boy here we go. This little pain in my ass has been through a lot with me. We have grown up together in this crazy household, but I certainly would not want to do it with anyone else. Zal, you are my best friend. We do sing-alongs and get into fist fights, all in the name of sibling love. He's a mischievous little one I'll tell you that.

Grandpa (*Aspi*): My grandpa is someone who cannot hurt a fly. Very few times have I seen him get really mad. He has had a hard life, always taking care of the people around him. There are very few people who have worked harder than him to provide a better life for others around him. He deserves the best.

Grandma (*Yasmin*):. Ahhh yes. One of my favorite people on this planet. This sarcastic and brutally honest woman has my heart. I do not know what I would do without her. I could listen to her tell stories over and over again. The best story-teller I ever met. Keep being your sassy self, we all know where I get it from ;)

Uncle (*Fred*): Last but not least. The man to thank for this entire book happening. Honestly when I was younger I saw him as kind of an outsider, a little weird ha ha. Although as I got older I realized everyone else was the odd one out. He is someone who really cherishes everything life has to offer. I most definitely look up to him, he's an inspiration. There is not enough gratitude in the world I can give him for everything he has done for me.

I will always be part of your lives.
All of you will always be part of my life.

INTRODUCTION

This book is not for other people. Really, it's selfishly for my very own self. This was really never meant to be a book. It was simply a collection of thoughts I wrote in my journal everyday. I wrote this book as a form of therapy to cope with each day and to try and have a purpose. I want to love the thing I create. And I might be too naive, too stubborn, or too young to realize what is the right thing to do, but I am willing to take the risk.

There are a lot of books written about teenagers nowadays, whether it's a fictional story of a love triangle between a girl, a vampire, and a werewolf or a nonfiction biography of an average teenager trying to survive high school. However, if you look up the authors of those books, you find they are written by middle-aged adults for whom being a teenager feels as more of a memory rather than a current reality. So, I thought it was time for a teenager to write about her point of view. What? A teenager, you say? Yes, and if you have a problem with that, feel free to put this book down and continue searching through the sea of books in your local library. However, I will tell you one thing before you decide to stay or go. Very few will tell you the truth about being a teenager; it's too depressing. I actually decided to do it because of slight depression and insomnia. This was my way to cope with it all.

This process has helped me in my journey, and now, I am putting this truthful story out in the world for two reasons. First and formost, in the hopes that it might give some hope to a teenager looking for the light at the end of the tunnel. Second, the adults around us might take the time to reflect and become aware of what we are truly going through at this phase of our lives. It's up to you if you want to read it.

If you are reading this paragraph, you probably decided to stay. Wow, thank you! That actually means a lot. So, you want the truth? You are sick of the lies, drama, and people simply not understanding what you deal with on a day-to-day basis - while you are stuck in an overcrowded building, a.k.a. high school? Here it is, the cold hard truth. Opinions welcome! We do not judge here.

I am here to tell you about all of the things

that I have heard over the course of my life. Although I have not lived for very long, I have been keeping track of things people have said throughout the years. I've been looking for those special "needle in a haystack" people. The ones that stand out from the crowd. The ones that think differently from the rest. Some things I say are my original ideas, but many ideas belong to the people around me.

Just listen, and you will be amazed by the things you hear; things that most people don't even notice.

This book is written for anyone who would like to know what a teenager thinks, feels, and wonders about life. Younger people might find useful ideas in this book, as well as a kindred spirit; while older people might find it very interesting to see what a teenager has to say to them and others, because the book offers a better understanding of the way younger people think, a useful reminder to anyone who might have forgotten.

00. My Opinion Before We Get Started

Dogs are better than cats. Mushrooms are disgusting. Pluto is not actually a planet. The world is round, the world is flat, eggs are good for you, eggs are bad for you...We are all full of opinions. Everyone thinks differently about the world and all the things that make it our world. That is the fantastical thing about opinions: no one can tell you if they are right or wrong (yes, I realized that I just said fantastical). Do you ever look around you and think: how did I get to this point in my life? What does the future hold in store for me? What will I do, who will I become? These are the questions that run through my mind. However, the biggest question I have about the society we live in today is simply: why? I question the choices that some people make in their lives, including my own decisions. I just want to know why, like that annoying seven year old who asks "why" all the time.

It's amazing how adults keep asking us «why» about the choices we make as teenagers, yet they have stopped asking themselves that very question about their own choices. I find that adults can't justify their choices, yet expect us to have insight into ours. It's not just adults, either. Many teens don't ask why, and they just go along with the flow without questioning it.

I fear that our civilization is too blinded by their busy lives to just stop and take it all in. Take a deep breath and close your eyes. Take a moment to think, because you only have one life. It would be a shame to waste it. I have a million different opinions and questions running through my head every day. So, I thought – why not share them? You can agree or disagree. Do whatever your heart desires. No one is telling you what to say or do; it's all up to you.

Just take the time to become aware of why you do what you do and say what you say.

01. A Life-Sucking Waste of Time Or (In Other Words) Our Lovely Education System

So, what is the point of school? To learn, right? Wrong. Sure, that was the original concept, but it's not what it is today. School was created thousands of years ago for the sole purpose of educating the people in a particular community. And for many years it stayed that way, until we arrived in a century where that all went to the back of our minds, and we created a different reason for school to exist. It's called getting good grades to get a good GPA to get into college to get more good grades to get another decent GPA only to end up in the recently crappy "real world". Sounds fun, right? Well, how can we fix this? That is a hard question. Any ideas, feel free to contact whoever the hell came up with the idea of this education system. Or at least the people who enforce it today.

It's not that I disagree with the idea of education. I see a lot of value in education. Learning can be great, it's just that the system is not run in a good way. We need to find a way to distribute knowledge in a better way. Could we fix it? See above.

Along with maintaining your grade point average, there are other responsibilities as well. While you are studying for hours, make sure you play a couple of sports, do volunteer work, play an instrument, join clubs, get at least 8 hours of sleep everyday, and - oh yeah - don't go completely insane. That totally makes sense. Oh, and an added bonus: you will probably not use any of these things in your daily life. Fun times. You don't know how to plan your finances, to write a check, pay taxes, put a down payment on a house, how to cook, how to clean, but it's okay, you at least know the freaking pythagorean theorem and that the mitochondria is the power house of the cell. Yup, that will definitely help you.

With this kind of training from an early age, it's no wonder adults forget how to slow down, how to smile, even how to get to know each other!

So, do you see the pattern of flaws yet? If not, I'll tell you the most unfortunate thing. There is a certain type of anxiety that a student feels when a bubble sheet determines their entire future. That anxiety results in hundreds of children across the world cheating, in turn, teaching them how to cheat through life itself. We are conditioned to fear failing, failing in life. This, ladies and gentlemen, is pathetic. Are you serious? Why would you want to put the future of your society through this?

We as teenagers are faced with planning our entire existence on this planet in a matter of years. We can't change our mind; we can't go back. We feel we can't go back, because our safe route gives us security, even if our emotional security suffers as a result. We lose our purpose. Ever wondered how rich people can be so rude? Probably because they are unhappy, as happiness is not measured by the number of dollar bills we have. It's just they did not think about their purpose before seeking riches and material things only.

So, we have to plan our entire future, while having to ask permission to go to the bathroom.

Seems reasonable... The thing about school is that everyone has to go through it. All these things are useless unless we are taught the purpose of them in our lives. The day they change the way we are educated will be a day when I am long gone or at least done with my schooling. There will come a day when I will be done with my education (but I will never be done with my learning). So, until that day comes: suck it up. Sorry, that was kind of harsh. But I feel you. I'm a teenager, and I am getting conditioned to hate life so much right now when all adults do is focus on these things and forget this is suppose to be fun along the way. It is honestly so exhausting I feel that I won't make it out alive. However, the day I do get out into the "real world" where I am free to make my own decisions is the day I will look back at all my hard work and know that I made it, that I did it for me.

I just hope I also look back and know I had fun along the way.

I feel that school should be better. Our teachers shouldn't teach us to think like them, but teach us to think for ourselves. They shouldn't teach us how to do well in school, but to do well in real life – we should learn how to communicate, how to chase our dreams without losing the ground beneath us, how to think and solve real problems, not just how to count apples and solve equations. They should teach us to keep our creativity, not take it away by enforcing a strict set of rules. I feel that a lot of us are lost, because we don't see the purpose in the things we do every day, mainly, school.

If we were shown a purpose in school, maybe we would not be so lost all the time?

02. Acceptance

You are here. Present in your own skin. You may not feel fully comfortable with yourself, your life, or your current situation. But forget all that, because the first step to accepting the people surrounding you is to learn to love yourself. Do not get stuck in your own thoughts, troubled by the fear of being happy for once. Yes, there is such a thing as being unhappy with yourself. I know it sounds crazy, but it happens. Things happen. Life happens. You can't change the life that has been planned for you. No, I am not talking about "destiny", I know we all make our own life choices, blah, blah, blah. Just try to be comfortable in your own skin, because everyone is unique in their own way. Tell yourself "I accept myself", "I'm frickin' fabulous", or whatever puts a smile on your face and makes you laugh a little. YOU ARE FABULOUS. Tell yourself that every day. Scream it from the rooftops. I promise that after some time your happiness will be contagious and spread through out your body and to others. Accept that you are beautiful, and nothing is going to change that. Live your life with pride and with hopes of a future filled with love and joy, because that is what every human being deserves in the end. This is what you deserve from this moment on. You are worth it.

The first step to accepting the people surrounding you is to learn to love yourself.

03. Accomplishments

Trophies, medals, and certificates for academics, sports, and many other things. These are symbols of our accomplishments. We should be proud of them. Not because we have these objects, but because of how we obtained them. The reason we do things shouldn't be for those prizes, but for the love of doing these things. By the time I finish high school, I want to achieve something. I want something to come out of my 12 years of education other than a slip of paper to mark my completion. I don't want my time spent turn out to be a waste. I want it to have substance. I think that is what I could also recommend to others – follow your dream. Not that cheesy dream you might have had, but that thing you really, really wanted to do, but then someone, maybe your college adviser or your parents said would be the wrong thing for you; that it would leave you starving. Do that thing.

I used to believe that my worth was measured by my accomplishments, by the things others gave to me.

I am now starting to realize that my worth and value does not come from the end results, but from how I lived my journey.

One day, I saw that my material prizes didn't give me much joy. Rather, I could get a lot more satisfaction out of the accomplishments I had made along the way. The path to success is not a sprint to the finish line, but a light jog that lets me take in the scenery.

Enjoying every moment, smiling,
living, no matter the outcome:
That's a real accomplishment.

04. Adulthood

An overrated concept, I might say. The circle of life in which the ones who were being told what to do are now doing the telling. As for adults, I would not use that word, rather, I see them as large children, just not as creative or open-minded, definitely more cynical. Adults have lost the child in them.

The good news is that bringing it back is simple! You know when you are a kid enrolled in a little league sport, and someone tells you to "be the ball?" That's what adults need to do. They need to "be the child", act like children in spirit. Just ask yourself: would a little kid think twice about doing what they love? Would they measure the amount of love they give others based on appearances? No. They would go for it, because they have nothing to lose. Adults, on the other hand, are too worried about their image, about what they will lose by acting a bit childish at times. What they don't realize is that they will only "tarnish their image" by how much they want to tarnish it. Nothing less, nothing more. Some of us think that when we grow up, we have to have it all together. The truth is, it may seem like people have their shit together, but that is so not true. Everyone is just trying to make it day after day. They will get there slowly, but surely. You see, these big children that are running our world today learn a lot from the actual children and the elders. They don't want to make the same mistakes as in the past, and they sure as hell want to make a good impression on the future generation, either that or our future is doomed for sure. 90% of people don't even know what they want to do, let alone know what they are good at! (I totally bullshitted that percentage, but it's a large percent, so bear with me). It might take 100 years to figure out what we were meant to do, and what we will love to do instead of our daily desk jobs. Yet, if we can have our dream job for just a couple of indulgent seconds, then we will have lived.

I would say some people know the truth, some people can admit being lost in life. Those are the people who are honest and express what they feel rather than faking it. They are the ones who know that there is no time for being two-faced, carrying the burden of a lie. Nothing good comes of it.

There is no time for being anything
other than yourself.
And part of yourself is the child within you.

05. Age is Just A Number. Right?

Of course it is. Numbers mean absolutely nothing when it comes to the number of human years that we live on this planet. Just because you're old, doesn't mean you're wiser, and just because you're young, doesn't mean you don't know anything. For ejemplo (that's "example" in Spanish. You learned something new today; you're welcome): take a 16-year-old and a 50-year-old (this might be a little extreme, but you'll get the point). The 50-year-old, pretty old in human years, has lived a long life, and has only ever left their house for groceries and the occasional stroll. The 16-year-old, young in human years, has only lived on the Earth for a short period of time, but this 16-year-old has been to the moon. Who's wiser? Well, it's up to you to figure it out. I only lead the horse to water; I will never force it to drink (sorry, had to put a cheesy line in there just for funzies). So, that's pretty much all I have to say about age.

Listen to your elders, and listen to your young, because you can learn many things from both groups.

Listening to your elders is wise, because they can share their stories and their journey with you, so maybe that will help you find your own journey.

How can adults learn from the young?
....the simplicity, the simplicity, the simplicity!!!

06. Airplanes

Invented by Orville and Wilbur Wright. A phenomenon that took the world by storm. People were intrigued over the future possibilities, but also scared of what this flying machine could do (I mean, I wasn't there, but I'm sure that's what people thought). Of course, today it has evolved into a trillion-ton metal flying machine that flies people across the world in a matter of hours, but if it weren't for those two broth- ers, we would have never been able to do what we do today. Just some food for thought.

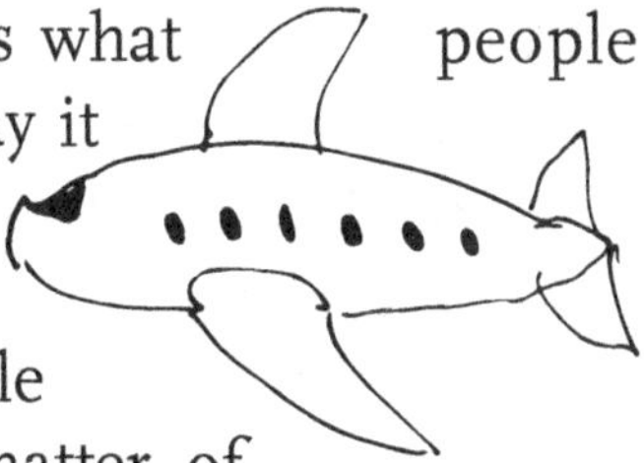

The brothers decided they could fly, and nobody could stop them. You can fly too, and you shouldn't let anyone clip your wings. Maybe you will create the next airplane, who knows?

You shouldn't let anyone clip your wings.

07. An End Game

The most important thing in your journey in figuring yourself out is that you have to have an endgame. You need something to look forward to. Setting small goals along the way is helpful. Something you want to accomplish can be achieved when you really want it. At the end of day, we all want to make it. We want comfort and stability, but we don't want to sacrifice our aspirations in order to do it. I know that sounds like a dream, and, unfortunately, it's not the current reality anymore for most. The American Dream has lost its sparkle, all too soon. We make our own dreams now. The dreams of the people. At times, in order to gain our perfect lives, we must sacrifice our comforts for a short period of time. Is it a gamble? Oh yes! 100%, definitely a gamble.

However, if you never try, how will you know?

08. Anxiety/Depression

Your heart is pounding, and you're hyperventilating, gasping for air. There is no one that can help you. You feel alone. No one can save you. The only person that can overcome this is you. This is a serious thing I see everyday, when I pass people in the halls and when I experience it myself. The worst thing that someone can go through is to feel like they are alone. When it's you and another person against the world, it feels good; you have someone who can take on the world with you. But when it's just you against the world (that's 7 billion people, I might add), it's frightening. You want to cry all the time, because you are in this state of nothingness. Uncontrollable sadness. Nothing sparks happiness and laughter in your body. You have forgotten what happiness feels like. And, when you have lost happiness, what is the point of living, right? WRONG. There is always a point to living, even if you can't find one at that moment. You can't give up. There are thousands of sick people who don't have the choice whether they live or die. You have a choice. Do not choose the wrong one (which would be killing yourself). Most of those 7 billion people in the world are probably going through the same thing. In the end it's not worth it. You are not worthless to me, so please stay.

There is always a point to living, even if you can't find one at that moment. You can't give up.

09. Arguments

A form of language that is very popular among our beloved congressmen and all politicians, and it will stay popular for another century or two. Like these congressmen, 99% of the time arguments go nowhere. They become pointless, nothing is resolved, and no one essentially wins or feels happy.

What's worse is that most arguments are misunderstandings, in my opinion. Someone takes something the wrong way, they get mad, the other person gets mad, and they argue. It's a vicious cycle. Parents who argue might teach it to their kids by example, especially when those children are in the "copycat" stage, the kids carry it on. It's situational, like life often is. That's why it's so hard to manage – no survival guide for life.

How about the way teenagers see adults communicate on a daily basis? Do you, our adult leaders, teach us how to communicate effectively or are you just like politicians of your own little world?

Most arguments are misunderstandings.

10. A Purpose

Some people believe that everyone on this planet has a purpose. Everyone has their calling. What they failed to mention is that not all these purposes are good. You could lead your purpose down the criminal road. Not everyone can be a famous celebrity or win a Nobel peace prize.

If you really want to strive to become famous, be my guest, but make sure you try to find your true purpose in life before you audition for the leading role.

I'm also not saying that you should find your inner serial killer. But consider all your options before you follow the crowd. Remember we learn about history to try and never repeat it. And if you were born before 2008, you were already Time Magazine's person of the year (in 2008 Time Magazine made everyone in the world their person of the year). So, that's an accomplishment right there, and you didn't even have to do anything. You have time to figure things out, so don't stress too much. Oh, and adults: Please stop pressuring your kids so much, allow them to breathe and find their path. It will do more damage than good. It's like trying to fix something that isn't broken; you're just making whatever it is worse. I have seen it happen with my own family members, how people can crack under pressure and develop some serious issues if they are pushed to their limits.

You have got time to figure things out, so don't stress too much.

11. Attitude

Wherever you go, whatever you do or accomplish in life, there is one thing to keep in mind. That is, first and foremost, your attitude, my friend. People will always remember if a specific person was mean, nice, sassy, rude, dumb, etc.

They will always remember the basic attitude you had towards them, and towards yourself.

Attitude is everything, my mom used to

say. Human beings with a good attitude about different things in life are guaranteed to have a more fulfilling and happy life (sounds like a commercial ad "guarantee", but I promise you that a good attitude costs nothing). So just do everything putting your best foot forward.

Don't let anything get you down or ruin your attitude. You are in control.

12. Be Polite

Have your parents ever told you to "treat others the way you want to be treated"? Yeah, me too. Well, listen to them! Manners are everything. If you are a kind person, you will go very, very far in the world. I guarantee it 100%. I don't freakin' care if you are the smartest person in the world, if you're not kind to others, then you will not get that far just by being "smart". One characteristic people seem to always notice is kindness, because it makes the person feel amazing.

If you are a kind person, you will feel peace inside of you.

13. Bored. Bored. Bored.

Lalalalalala. Oh. My. Gosh. I am so so so so so bored. I'm so bored at this point that I would do anything. Ever feel like this? Yeah, well, I am currently mentally dying from boredom. Usually I go online looking for things to do. So far I have talked to myself, talked to the neighbor's dog, thoroughly embarrassed myself in front of the neighbor, and done a bunch of other things. Then it hit me. Maybe when I am busy and wishing for something else to do, I should write it down. That way when I have the time, I will have a list of things to do. Smart, eh? I think so. I am going to find something moderately productive to do now. You should do the same! It only benefits you. Let's make a list together.

Get a pen and paper out right now and make a list you can keep adding things to.

14. Bucket Lists

Everyone has one. That checklist filled with personal things you want to do before you die, most of them consisting of cliches, such as skydiving and blah, blah, blah. You want to make sure you lived your life to the fullest no matter what. There's no way in hell you are leaving this world with regrets. No way. However, I'll tell you one thing: your bucket list does not have to please others. Just you. If you are afraid of heights, you don't have to go skydiving! Unless you want to, not because others tell you you should. Make your own list. Like I want to eat chocolate cake without feeling guilty or I want to laugh so hard that I pee my pants. You have full control of what you put on that list.

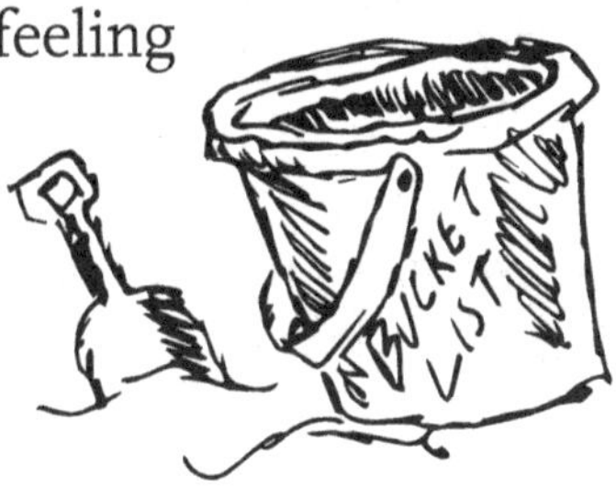

Your bucket list does not have to please others. Just you.

15. Bus Rides

Public transportation is used when you cannot get a ride from someone or you can't drive. Most people choose to ride the bus because it is the best option in their life at that point. Although it might be a pain, especially if you are the first stop in the morning or the last stop in the afternoon, you will always meet new and interesting people – if you allow yourself to do so. It's fun to get to know someone new and learn new things you did not know about. Be open-minded wherever you go. You will never learn something new every day if you are not open to learning new things from a variety of people.

Be open-minded with people wherever you go.

16. Cellphones

The revolutionary device that allows you to communicate with those who are somewhere else or, for some people, those sitting right next to you, because you would rather text them than talk face-to-face. The cellphone's original purpose was to communicate, yet it failed to do just that, since people prefer to call their next-door neighbor over just walking 10 feet to talk to them in person. Or they prefer to have a whole middle-school relationship through texts over having awkward conversations in person. Einstein predicted it. He said: "I fear the day that technology will surpass our human interaction. The world will have a generation of idiots." So, prove him wrong!

Put the phone down once in a while and have a conversation with someone.

Don't get me wrong, technology is great, but the one thing that it should not do is consume our lives. If you are always looking down at a small chunk of metal and plastic in your hand, you'll miss the big picture.

Get disconnected off your phone and go connect with someone.

17. Changing the World

Most people choose to be cliché and say they aspire to change the world. If you are one of those people, no offense, but you are annoying. Don't take it too personally, I mean no offense. But, honestly, you want to change the world? What's wrong with it? Okay, point taken. There are a lot of things wrong with it. However, I believe it does not need to be changed. This little-and-big world we live in just needs some guidance to push it in the right direction, whether you are the person to do that or not. We need a little less sadness in our routine and a lot more happiness and kindness.

So, you want to change the world? Then spread happiness and kindness, and you're there.

People don't change, they just haven't unlocked their hearts. Some people have a harder time than others on unlocking that pesky thing (yup, our hearts are pretty pesky). Alright, you want to change the world? Then go, but do it the right way. You don't have to cure cancer to feel accomplished. It's the little things that really matter in life. Your choice. It's always your choice, no matter what.

So, you want to change the world?
Then spread happiness and
kindness, and you made it!

18. Choices

From time to time, we have to make tough decisions. We have to decide what we want and what is important to us. It's different for everyone. Everyone has different priorities. You have to be the one to decide. It's up to you and you only. Even if the decision that we make is against everyone's wishes, against what our families and friends think we should do. Who cares? It's not their life. It's yours!!! They are a

part of your life, but they most certainly do not own it. Take control and make that tough decision, or forever hold your peace! You should be accountable for yourself, even if you don't see that accountability in others, like some adults or teachers. Their lives are their own, too, so speak for yourself and make yourself accountable.

There comes a time we have to decide what we want and what is important to us.

19. Christmas/Hanukkah/Kwanzaa/Whatever you celebrate over the holidays

Unless you are the Grinch, Christmas or the Holidays are your favourite time of year. The only time we can be both stressed and joyful at once. Usually, we are stressing over what presents to buy and for whom. We are also joyful, because we will be spending time with our families. However, if you are a senior in high school about to apply for college or a single 30-year-old, getting together with the family might not be your favourite activity. Your family will probably never stop being nosy and getting into your business all the time. Let them do it, they had to go through it with their parents, so it is their turn now. You will have your time later on.

Still trying to find the perfect gift for that special someone, a family member, or even for a secret Santa? Don't stress about it. If they are truly your friend, they will not care what you get them as long as it comes from the heart. After all, Christmas is not about presents.

It's about spending time with family and friends, nothing more and nothing less.

20. College Applications

What are you majoring in? Where are you going? When? How? Why? Are you sure? Sounds familiar: the most annoying and stressful thing you could go through. Your whole family is bombarding you with questions you have no answers for. You try to avoid large family gatherings to avoid that topic of conversation. At some point, you just feel like a broken record. No worries, it will soon be over. Once you get into a college, you will experience a great feeling of accomplishment as a reward for all your hard work. Or, maybe, the lack of hard work if no college accepts you. Either way, you will be done. You will move onto another chapter of your life, and that will be the end of that. Maybe you wished the situation was different, but don't just go through the motions as that is not living. Do the things you don't want to do to get into the places you want to be. So hang in there!

Don't just go through the motions
as that is not living.

21. Color

Everyone will say that something is right there in black and white, implying that is clearly stated right in front of your eyes, that all the answers to your questions are right in front of you. But, thing is, our world is in color, because of the pigment in our eyes and the way we see objects around us. Hold up. I thought that all the answers were right in front of us, in black and white? Well, the world is in color, so I guess you will just have to make your own answer. It's up to you. There is no right or wrong. No black and white. Just color to brighten your day and make everything just a little bit better. Without color our lives would be a boring place. Everyone knows the answers, but no one wants to share. Color can mix together to create new colors; the ability to share your answers and create new ones with the people around you. Now that's magical.

Slow down and notice the colors around you.

22. Complication

Hello, my dear readers. I am here to tell you a secret. A secret that people may think of, but not know how to say. When we have a moment of dissatisfaction, and people ask us what's wrong, we usually reply with: "It's complicated". The thing we forget is that life is simple. When life feels compliated one of two things are happening. We are just compliating things in our minds, or we allow the people in our lives to make it complicated.

You are your own person. Live simply.

23. Compliments

As human beings, we do not yet have the ability to read minds, so we are subjected only to our own thoughts. I know, so unfair, right? When we are out in public, there tends to be a lot of people around. All of us are in the same place, but it's almost like we are by ourselves, because everyone is on their own, doing their own thing. When we see people sitting alone, we try to guess what they could be thinking. At least I do. I feel bad. Maybe they went through a bad break-up, a family death, or they're just alone, doing nothing, are perfectly fine, and in no way sad at all! Who knows. Either way, they are alone, and no one should be alone unless they are watching Netflix or are on the toilet. So, just a suggestion; go up and compliment them on their clothes or whatever. The dialogue could go something like this:

"Hey there! I was just walking and saw your shirt. It's super cute, where did you get it?"

"Oh, this old thing? Just at this one store."

"Wow! Well it looks really nice on you. Just wanted to mention that."

"Thanks!"

Exit stage to left or right with a kind smile directed to person that you are leaving

Their mood is 100% guaranteed to have changed into a better one. They might look at you weird or tell you to piss off. Hey! You tried, and that's what counts. Who cares how they take it? You might think that in the moment you did nothing to improve the world in any way. However, the thing is... you did! A changed mood sets the tone for everyone that particular person runs into during the day. It is a scientifically proven fact (yes, really, no bullshit) that when a person sees another with a good attitude or a bright smile, they tend to reciprocate the same happy feelings. The same happens with a bad attitude and a frown. It's sort of contagious and can travel great distances. Technically, now you can say you made a difference in the atmosphere around you. Be proud of yourself for once, because you deserve it. Worst case is that you will feel good and your day will be brighter.

A simple compliment not only
makes others feel amazing,
it also makes you shine from the inside.

24. Crying

Liquid happiness comes out of your right eye first. Liquid sadness comes out of the left eye first. Most of the time, we cry when we are sad. We are broken by something someone has done or said to us. Some are stronger than others and rise above it. Some think they are too tough to cry. Some have felt pain for a lost loved one. Some find it weird that this is what happens to us. Whatever you feel when you cry, everyone has felt it too. So, I guess what I am trying to say is: no matter who you think you are or what you are going through, you have to let it out, because if you keep it in, one day you will explode with emotions and won't be able to control yourself. If you want to be alone, then leave and cry. But don't pity yourself. Everyone is strong in their own way.

You are strong and can get through anything,
if you allow youself to just be and
let it all out once in a while.

25. Curiosity

As kids, curiosity is about the only thing we have as an advantage over our elders. They have wisdom and more life experience and blah, blah, blah. But we've got a powerful thing. You see, we believe the world is huge, when in reality it's actually quite small compared to the universe it lives in. I mean, we want to know everything, because we're not all grown up. Let me tell you that no one will know everything. The point is that we can't lose this curiosity. Once we lose the feeling of being curious, we lose interest. And once we lose interest, we lose purpose. And once purpose is lost, well, we're just going through the motions and living out our days until we go to the other side. If you're reading a book and don't understand something, look it up. If you are wondering how to bake something, bake it. Create something. All you have to do is look it up with a click of the mouse. After all, everyone is saying that all the answers are on the Internet now.

It's endless. Just like your curiosity should be.

26. Dare To Be Different

Unless you're an undercover agent or a ninja, you don't want to blend into the crowd. Everyone wants to be different in their own way to stand out, so find the special thing that will make you stand out. If everyone was the same, it would be extremely boring! Do you want to be boring? Yeah, didn't think so. Nobody does. Be yourself, and if people want to criticize, critique, or try to fix you, screw them! They are boring, remember that! Never lose sight of who you are, even if someone is blocking your view. Just push them out of your way. If someone can't accept you for who you are, then they are not worth your very precious and limited time on Earth.

Never lose sight of who you are, even if someone is blocking your view.

27. Daylight Savings Time

Either the days are turning shorter and brighter, or they are becoming long and dark. There is the one day in the world where everyone changes the time on their clocks (or has a phone that completes the task for them). You either gain an hour of sleep or lose it; something that will definitely be determining your mood for the rest of that day. If you're gaining an hour, make the most of it just for that day. If you are losing an hour, well, an hour isn't that long anyway, so...

...don't worry too much or get too cranky.

28. Deep Breaths

Deep breaths are like a reset button for your mind and soul. Take a deep breath in... and out. It feels good. Like you're lifting a weight off your shoulders. Letting everything go. Try it when you need to hit the reset button and start fresh.

Your breath is connected to every part of your physical and mental state.

29. Don't Be Sad

Are you frustrated? Are you sad? If so, it is okay to be. It is healthy to be connected to all your emotions. But do not let them control you. Would you like a reason not to be sad? Sure, I would be happy to give you many. If you are a teenager: you need to be happy, because you are the future; there is no future without you. Middle-Aged adult: you are the current society, so you can't slip up. An elder: you set the example for the world that we live in today, yeah, that was you, so you should pat yourself on the back instead of being depressed and sad.

Allow yourself to feel, but do not let your feelings rule you.

30. Don't Settle

Many (successful) adults will tell you what they did to get to where they are now. They will proceed to share their thoughts on how you should do the same. Things will come up, such as "You want to have a comfortable life", "Get a job that will give you the money, and then you'll be able to do the things that you actually want to do", "You don't have to like what you are doing for a living, as long as you receive a substantial profit". This is all wrong. Terrible advice, people!

You should love your job so much that when you retire, you will be able to say that you have never worked a day in your life.

Of course, that is incredibly hard, since your dreams might be against your parents wishes. But it's your life, not theirs. If you want to do something, then don't let anyone walk all over you, as you will most definitely regret it later. Be open to truly listening to the advice of your family and those you trust, but in the end it is your life you will be living. Some of us are afraid due to finances and security. That our dreams may not make it out there in the real world. Hey. Let me tell you something. Although it might be terrifying, if you are passionate about your dream and work hard to achieve it, everything else will fall into place. Children should be free to go follow their dreams no matter what the cost, and parents should encourage them as much as possible.

You should love your job.
Yes, it is that simple.

31. Eating

Many people have a love for food. This includes me. It's not just a necessity to me, I enjoy eating whatever it may be. Unfortunately, some people are too scared to eat, because they are worried about what they look like. Well, here's a secret: no matter if you are a boy, or a girl, or both, or an alien:

Healthy is beautiful!

Whatever healthy looks like shouldn't matter. The important thing is to love your body no matter its shape. Sometimes people cannot help their appearance, because of an illness or family genetics. If you are living a healthy life, you are beautiful (yes, I had to say it twice for emphasis). It's simple: be happy and be healthy, and that's it, no added complications. I think you're beautiful, and I don't even know you, but what I do know is that you are awesome because:

1. You are reading this amazing book :)
2. If you are being yourself, no one can criticize you. I will leave it at that.

The important thing is to love your body no matter its shape.

32. Exhausted

I am so tired. Tired of trying to please people that will never be pleased. Tired of the countless hours I give, only for them not to pay off. Tired of people telling me I'm not trying hard enough or that I am doing everything wrong. I am tired, but... I am not going to let the agonizing pain I feel every day to stop me from doing what I want to do and being who I want to be. Because if I did, if I let myself break down and get angry, then I would have lost sight of my true goals and more importantly, who I am as a person. So, I tune the negativity and self absorbed people out. My main focus is myself and my own path. I don't care about anyone else's path. They can rise to the top, have successful lives, and become billionaires. Good for them. As for me, I will pave my own path that will lead me to where I want to go.

You are drained and don't think you can do more. Dig deeper. Tap into that part of your mind you have never tapped into before. That is what makes an individual stronger. That's when people look at someone and say: "Wow, that person is brave as hell, I wish I could be like that."

Tap into the part of your mind you have never tapped into before.

33. Everything's Going To Be Okay

Are you completely exhausted? Tired all the time no matter how much sleep you get? Yeah, me too! You could agree with me on this no matter what age you are. Everyone is tired. Everyone is confused, asking whether it's their life choices or their actual lives. Don't worry, you're not the only one who feels this way. You're not alone. Everything will turn out okay. Even if you believe it won't be okay, everything happens for a reason, it's just you don't know the reason in the moment.

Everything passes, in time it will be okay.

34. Family

I consider family to refer not only to those people who are related to you by blood, but also to fellow companions who are always there for you no matter what. Really, what matters in the end is the people who are left by your side when everything goes wrong. There might only be one person who stands by your side, but one is all you need. Sure, more would be nice, but if you have at least one person there for you at all times, you're doing pretty well. The thing is, everyone has family drama. I do not believe for one second someone has a perfect family with no drama. If you don't have any family drama yet, then, oh boy, be ready for something huge to go down or for a big family secret to appear, trust me. Although we have all this drama in our families, they will be there for you when no one else is, so appreciate the ones who stay no matter what and focus less on the people who leave you, as they are simply not worth it.

What matters in the end is the people who are left by your side when everything goes wrong.

35. Feminism

A common word used today. Whether it is in social media, the news, a celebrity talk show, or a conversation with someone making fun of it. Honestly, I believe that feminism is an irrelevant subject to talk about. The definition of feminism is: the advocacy of women's rights on the grounds of political, social, and economic equality to men. Basically, women want to be treated equally to men. But the only thing that awareness of feminism is doing is creating jokes and showing weakness in women. All women are doing is protesting. If you really want to be equal, stop the talking and consistently keep doing what you need to do. And guys: shut up and grow up. Women are just as good as you are, so stop being so full of yourselves. The key to living happily is to live in harmony with one another. So do that and see what happens. I mean, we have tried everything else.

The key to living happily is living in harmony with one another.

36. Follow the Signs

Our minds do tricky things from time to time. One day we'll be thinking of a random object, and suddenly we start to see it everywhere. Our brain notices things that we weren't even paying attention to before we thought of it. When you are looking for slug bug cars to punch someone in the shoulder, you start seeing a surprisingly large amount of those cars that you didn't notice before. Maybe you want to join the army, and you keep seeing recruiting signs around town. No matter what you are thinking of, you seem to feel that it is a coincidence you keep seeing these "signs". The truth of the matter is that this thing has always been there, you have just started to notice it now. If this keeps happening to you, I suggest you follow your gut and go through with it.

What you consistently think of will
become part of your daily life.

37. Freshman

Ahh, freshman year... I remember it like it was yesterday, or, at least, that's the common phrase used when talking about nostalgia for the past, although my freshman year wasn't necessarily nostalgic. I mean, it was great: I was out of middle school, coming into a bigger school, meeting new people. I was the new fish in a big aquarium trying to maneuver my way around this mysterious place. My high school was insanely huge, so they added two extra minutes between classes just so that kids could get to their class on time. The freshmen were always teased by the upperclassmen and the occasional obnoxious sophomore that was literally just a freshman three months ago. During your first year in high school you are finding yourself, as it's a journey of transitioning and discovering new opportunities. It's fun for a while, but, man, you feel really happy when you are finally done being a freshman, that's for sure.

Never forget, you were there once as well.
So be kind to those who are there now.

38. Friendship

That's one of the main problems today. People are only thinking about themselves. It's rare that people do things out of the goodness of their hearts. You see love all around you. People getting engaged, married, having children. That is because there's something in it for both of them. They both get love. Never thought love would be so selfish, did you? How often do you see long-lasting friendships? Think about your best friend. If you are in a relationship with them or married to them, it doesn't count. I mean a friend that is always there for you no matter what. Well, what's in it for them? You don't get a prize for being someone's friend. That's the thing about friendship – there isn't anything in it for anyone.

People always want the answer to things. Tests, puzzles, riddles. Well, here's the key. Keep one of your friends close. All you really need is one true friend – everyone else is simply an acquaintance. My dad told me that and I will never forget it.

Keep one of your friends close. All you really need is one true friend.

39. Frustration

This is definitely one of the worst emotions you can feel. It is one thing to feel mad, but frustration is anger plus not being able to do anything about it. Whether no one believes you on a certain issue or they just don't get what you are trying to say, you become incredibly annoyed. When this happens, there is only one thing to do. Cool off. Right now you are too heated to interact with anyone, so walk away. After you have gathered your thoughts, do something else to get your mind off of things, because if there is nothing you can do about it, then it's not worth thinking the same thing over and over.

Frustration cannot exisit in a state of clarity. Allow yourself a break and you will be able to see your situation clearer.

40. Funerals

There will come a time in our life when the journey ends. Our life comes to a close. We hope to be remembered or forgotten. Either way, we have served our time and lived a life. Whether it was bad or good, it is over. Weird, huh? How it can all end just like that? I mean, maybe you die in your sleep, painless, but alone. Or you die doing a death-defying trick that will go in the Guinness World Records as a legacy that will never die (no pun intended). If you haven't already, one day you will sit down and write your will (basically saying which lucky family member gets your fortune), maybe plan your funeral. Some want a regular funeral, nothing special, just the generic way anyone would get buried or cremated. Others want a party to celebrate their death. Forget the tissues, they want a rager. Personally, I want both.

Gasp! Both, you say?! Yes. But how? Well, in the beginning people will cry, because obviously I will be sadly missed J, and then they will have a party. Also, no black clothes. Everyone must wear rainbow, tie dye, anything colorful, really. In addition to that request, no flowers either. Flowers die, and I mean, come on, it's a funeral, do we really need something else dying? Instead I demand teddy bears. They last forever. I mean, seriously forever. Something different. I do not necessarily want to be remembered.

But as long as I lived happy, there
will be nothing that I regret.

41. Generosity

The one thing that you should do in your lifetime, even if you do nothing else. You should give back. You don't have to go to Africa and save millions of lives (although that would be pretty cool). Just start off in your own community. Help is needed in every city and town. Each place goes through its own struggles, and you live in those places, feeling those struggles. So, help make that place a little bit better. Volunteer. I think it's the most rewarding thing ever.

But not just because it looks good on your college applications. It should be out of the kindness of your own heart. Too many things are done nowadays expecting something in return. There's always a catch. Someone always wants something. So be different. It not only betters your community, but it makes you feel good.

You want to be known for something?

Help out on a project where you get nothing in return, and you'll see that your small effort is making a big difference in the lives of some people. It means so much more to them that someone out there cares for them enough to help them at no cost. Restore our faith in humanity and go do something you can be proud of yourself for. You don't have to go to a poverty stricken village to make a difference, although that would be amazing. You can help right where you are, because people, big and small, old and young, need help everywhere.

Restore our faith in humanity and go do something you can be proud of.

42. Getting Off Topic

Many people believe that when you're writing you should always stay on topic. Well, I find that all kinds of boring! Once you talk about the same thing over and over again, you get tired of it. Anything repeated too many times becomes boring no matter what. Staying on topic kills your creativity. You won't be able to venture off and think about other things. I can tell you the best discussions tend to veer off topic, because you are looking at every aspect and angle of that particular topic. That's what sets someone apart, turning them from ordinary to extraordinary. So, if you're in an environment where topic doesn't matter, think different things all at once, but not too much – we wouldn't want your head to explode. :)

Staying on topic kills your creativity.

43. Graduation

Done. Finished. It's all over. You are finally done with the torturous hours of homework, studying, and being constantly worried about your impending future. But your worries are over, my friend, because you are committed to something and, for once in your life, you know what you are doing. Enjoy it while it lasts. The sense of accomplishment is immensely great, and you are worthy of it. Go out and party your ass off. But not too hard. Move your tassel from one side to the other, throw it up, and smile! Whoooooo. Goooooooo. Runnnn, because you have completed your school sentence. Maybe you didn't believe you could do it, but you did! Doesn't it make you feel more confident? Take advantage of that confidence boost – guide yourself to where you want to be.

The sense of accomplishment is immensely great, and you are worthy of it.

44. Grandparents

If you are lucky enough and your grandparents are still alive, make the most of it. They will only be there for so long. Ask them questions about their past. Ask them for stories. They have lived a long life, and they have plenty of wisdom to share – all they need is someone to listen. So listen. It will help you in ways you cannot even imagine. Their stories are sad, happy, and crazy at times. They will even tell you things about your parents that you had no idea about. You will learn about your true family history in order to pass on to your family. Every grandparent dreams that their children and grandchildren will care and cherish their stories and their relationship. For many, that is the only light their lives really have. It's the saddest thing when kids get too busy for their grandparents, because when they do find time, it's usually too late.

The greatest gift you can give
them is the gift of listening.

45. Growing Up

There is this constant need in children – they want to grow up. We are so concerned about getting older that we forget about the years in between. We tell ourselves we just have to get through the annoying hard part, and then we will be fine. Home free to be older. But is it really home free? Once we become older, sure, we have a certain amount of freedom in the sense that no one can tell us what to do. However, with this comes a price of taxes, a mortgage, taking care of your car when it breaks down, and fending for yourself in every aspect. No worries, at least your older, right? It's what you have been waiting for your entire life, yet it feels so unsatisfying. Along the way you might have lost your path. Gone in another mysterious direction that didn't have such a great outcome. You didn't follow your dreams because you wanted a comfortable life. You now have a comfortable life, but you regret your decision of giving up the one thing you longed to do. We get so caught up making a living that we forget to actually live. Hey, you know the picture perfect family? Yeah, me neither. That's because it doesn't exist. And if you believe you can make one, you are seriously misguided. If you are too busy spending time and effort creating the "setting" of the perfect picture, you might realize the loved ones you wanted to be there are no longer there.

Don't get so busy making a living that you forget to live and connect with your loved ones.

46. Gun Violence

Listen. I understand. It's a constitutional right, so suddenly when those rights are threatened, our patriotic side comes out. However, with the great responsibility that a gun implies come major consequences. Don't believe me? Well, let's take a little trip to the news, shall we?

Mass shootings, police brutality, guns, guns, guns, deaths, deaths, and more deaths. You do not fight fire with fire, so why are we fighting guns with more guns? Does that make any freaking sense?? That is what I do not understand. I am not stupid, I know we cannot get rid of the 9 billion guns spread across the U.S. We cannot confiscate guns from every single individual. But the least we can do is stop the people on the terrorist watch list from buying guns at their local store. Seem reasonable? I think so. Prayers for the victims of gun violence are no longer helping. Some type of legislation must be put in place for the repetitive madness to stop.

I encourage everyone to speak up in some way, shape, or form. Do not let shootings and that "life just isn't always fair" bull crap justify the fact that guns are okay. Do not let it cloud your judgment, you are better than that. Guns kill people, people kill people, at the end of the day, I don't give a shit. It's all violence and it needs to stop.

The more peace everyone shares,
the less room there is for violence.

47. Halloween

No matter what age you are, anyone can enjoy the holiday of eating candy till your stomach hurts, partying in costumes, or even passing out treats. Everyone is doing something festive. If you are not doing anything to celebrate, then you are celebrating by doing nothing. Halloween is the day to wear whatever you want, and no one is allowed to judge because you are free to express yourself. It is pretty cool. We will always look back at old pictures and remember what our interests were at that specific time in our life.

Although it's also an excuse to dress like a slut, but if that makes you feel good about yourself, then by all means go ahead. It saddens me to see how teenage girls find their worth in life throuh their bodies. But can you blame them? Everywhere you turn, all media, movies, shows, adults walking around; all of it shows to us kids that our worth should be based on our bodies.

You are never too old to dress up and have fun with your imagination.

48. Happiness

Everyone's ultimate goal in life is to find happiness in what they are doing in their daily lives. Although happiness sounds like a simple concept, there is one obstacle that you must overcome before you reach that state of being. That challenge is finding what makes you happy. If you find that thing/things, you are set for life. The only problem is that it might take a while to figure out what makes you happy. So, if you feel sad right now, or out of place, or even if you feel like you are just living with no purpose, go out and find your happiness. I'm not saying it will be easy, but I will say it is going to be great no matter what. Happiness does not come from a single situation. It has many elements. It comes with being grateful for what you have. It comes with making the best of every situation. It comes with the hope of finding one's passion some day.

Never lose sight of the simple things in life that make you happy – that means you are living your life.

49. HATE

Have you ever despised anything or anyone? Should I even utter the word hate? Hate is a strong word, I was once told by my uncle who hates the word hate. Well, actually he just really dislikes the word (see what I did there?). He always said, «hate is like drinking poison and hoping your enemy dies.» He says it's a very negative word, and, man, is he a positive guy (a little weird too, but weird is good... most of the time). Can't have hate and war, man, just peace and love (at least that's what hippies say, so I'm going with it). So, make love, not war, folks. Take in a deep breath of fresh air and let it all out or punch a wall, do what you want to deal with anger. You just do it and worry about everyone else another day. Hate = stress, so instead of hating something or specifically someone just forgive. You don't have to forget what they did to make you angry with them or hate them (ooooh, I said the H-word), just forgive and move on, because shit happens, and you just gotta deal with it. Move past it, clear your mind, and be at peace, because your life is always going to be better than another person's somewhere in the world. And in order to have a good life, you need a peaceful mind. Peace and love, no hate allowed. Hate wears us down. It's like drinking poison, a burden we never put down and that affects every area of our lives.

Move past it, clear your mind, and be at peace.

50. Have Dreams And Goals

It's important to have dreams and goals. Even if you think it's ridiculous, you never know what could happen. I dream that one day I will figure out what I want to do with my life. What do you aspire to be or to become? Future Goals: (you fill in the blank). It doesn't even have to be far into the future.

Think of what makes you happy,
what you want to experience,
who you want to become,
and then do it!

51. Here and Now

I've heard a lot about planning for the future lately. All this talk about what college are you going to attend? What are you planning to do with the rest of your life? If you are reading this, you are either thinking to yourself "yup, been there, done that", or, if you're a little younger, you don't know what I'm talking about, so enjoy that feeling because as you get older, you will have to carry more responsibilites and decisions. People never live in the moment. They are constantly worried about what their future will look like, what it will be. Will I die young? Or become a vampire and live forever? Stop, just stop, shut it down. Shut down the worries and emotions, because if you spend your whole life planning and worrying about your future, you're gonna miss out. Life will fly by, and you will have guaranteed regrets that you didn't live in the moment and didn't take things as they come. Trust me. Live in the now and deal with the rest later.

Cherish every moment.

52. I Am Kinda Tired

The most common word in a teenager's vocabulary is tired. We are tired of school, tired of family on certain occasions, tired due to lack of sleep, tired of drama, tired of judgement, tired of life. Can you believe that we have not even lived half our lives, and we are already tired? Yeah, I cannot believe it either. I am tired too. And the amount of times I have said tired in this paragraph is not even half of what a typical teenager would use throughout an entire day. However, it's okay, we are supposed to be exhausted for the rest of our teenage lives and then work our asses off so we are able to enjoy our future. Nobody gets everything they want handed to them from birth, unless you are a Kardashian. One day you will look back and know that your hard work has paid off. And that will be an unforgettable feeling.

Do not lose sight of all the gifts life has provided you just because you are tired.

53. I Am Lost

Yes. I am lost and searching for answers, signs, anything really, anything that will give me a sense of direction. A place to go or a journey to discover. Two-thirds of the world's population do not know what they want to do with their life. Even worse, those same people have no idea what they are good at or even capable of. Isn't that kind of sad? Yeah, it is. So what do we do? How do we find our way back? Or were we always lost... never meant to be found or discovered (oh yeah, I can get super poetic at times, you will see). I guess, like all things, time will tell. Do we have to be found? Not really. Do we have to know where we are going? Nope. At times, allow yourself to be lost, because that´s where the adventure is. We can enjoy the journey of being lost rather than forcing ourselves (and letting adults force us) to always have answers. Don't allow yourself to be found unless you want to.

Allow yourself to be lost, because that´s where the adventure is.

54. Keep The Creativity

Society seems very robotic nowadays. There is no creativity! What happened?! Why have we chosen just one type of thinking? One way or no way. Well, it shouldn't be like that. People say you should think outside the box, but I feel that people have lost the meaning of that phrase. When someone says one thing, think of it from a different point of view. Who knows what you could unlock in your brain? The possibilities are endless.

Just get rid of the box entirely
to free your creativity.

55. Kindness

Anyone ever tell you that the "real" world was this big scary place, everyone for themselves? Yeah, well... I don't think so. I might not have seen enough of the world to know, but I know it's not as big and scary as people make it out to be. We've got 7 billion people in the world. That means we've got 7 billion opportunities to be kind to someone. Help an elderly lady cross the street. Go give your worst enemy a genuine compliment just to see their confused reaction. Do something kind, helpful, something you wouldn't normally do. Don't do it so that other people can give you a pat on the back, do it for you. That's the difference between an act of kindness and just being nice. You are most likely going to get a pat on the back for being nice. When you do an act of kindness, it comes from the heart and genuinely makes you feel good, no reward needed. Your reward becomes the smile and appreciation on someone's face. And if they don't appreciate it, well... who cares? You know you did an act out of the kindness out of your heart. Nobody needs to justify their kind heart.

The most attractive character trait is kindness.

56. Labels

Black, White, Gay, Bisexual, Transgender, Asian, Indian, Bipolar, Christian, Jewish, Feminist, etc., etc. These words do not define a person. Your personality and the way you treat others are the things that define you as a human being. It's sick that this is even a problem in our society. The way we judge people on the things that we hear through other people or just on what we think ourselves. It hurts that we cannot accept people for who they are. We tell everyone to be themselves, to be who they are. How can we let human beings do that if we are just going to criticize them for it? How is that fair? I know the often used line "life isn't fair", but this is cruel. To give someone false hope is the worst thing you can do. Everyone is unique in their own way, but there is one thing that we all have in common: being human.

By not interacting with someone because of their beliefs or because of them being who they are, you are limiting yourself in terms of the endless possibilities of knowledge, friendship, or even love. When you label someone, you're not just hurting that person, but you are also hurting yourself. You are not experiencing the entire world if you are only interacting with part of it. So don't hurt yourself or the people around you any longer. Fight against the cruelty, and I promise you will be forever grateful you did.

Do you get it? We were all put here for a reason, right? Well, there is a reason for everything, whether it's known or unknown. The point is: God or the universe (which ever one you believe in) has put us here for a purpose. I am not quite sure if everyone has figured out what they were put here to do, but only time will tell. The thing is, we are all figuring stuff out, we're all scared. However, if we knew that the people around us would accept us for who we are then nobody would be scared anymore. We could find more opportunities to be happy... That would be nice. So, think about it next time you criticize someone for being who they are. Get to know them if you want, but you have no place to judge. Nobody can be perfect no matter how hard someone tries (or even how many surgeries they have); it is impossible. Unfortunately, if you think there is a way to become perfect, then you are losing sight of what is really important in life.

This is about being kind to others, whoever they may be. You want to change the world? Your acceptance towards someone is a step in the right direction.

The way you treat others defines
you as a human being.

57. Loneliness

No one is close to you. No one seems to care that you are here. At some point in your life, you feel alone. You just feel a void or an overall emptiness. No one seems to get you. You might be too unique for people. Or too far off. Oh no, you should not be sad about this. You are at a point where you are looking for genuine people. People that will be there for you. Do not settle for anything less than that. You won't be lonely forever, I guarantee that. There are 7 billion people in the world. All you have to do is go and talk to one.

Never give up on others, never give up on yourself.

You won't be lonely forever.

58. Looks

Thr first observation that we make when meeting a person is about the way they look. That is the first part of them we encounter. We see a large man: big muscles and a body covered with tattoos. Some of us might think, oh, that man must be a thug, he must steal stuff, he is probably a lowlife. Now you might be right, but you also might be wrong!! He might major in poetry. Or he might be a successful billionaire. (I exaggerate sometimes, only to get my point across). Then you walk down the street some more and run into a woman you met at church. You think very highly of her, because she worships god and probably has her life together. And you might be right, but you also might be wrong again!! She might be a cold-blooded killer who has murdered five people, and is responsible for many bank heists. (Again, exaggerating for effect) The point is, you don't know who you are dealing with until you give someone a chance. Just because your daughter's boyfriend has a motorcycle doesn't mean he is a criminal. Just because a girl in your class wears loads of make-up doesn't mean she's a slut who wants attention. Until we use our other senses, we have no right to judge or profile that person. What do you think people might think of you? Doesn't matter. As long as you are a kind person, you can get as many tatoos and put as much make-up on as you wish. Because no one has the right to criticize your character. Once people get to know one another, there won't be anymore confusion and misconceptions. Just be kind.

Be who you want to be. The rest
will take care of itself.

59. Lost

When I was little, I loved to get lost. No matter where it was or how it was: in the woods, in a big city, by myself, or with some of my friends. I just wanted to get lost and discover new things. I thought it was fun, even exciting. But then I inevitably grew up, and being lost no longer sounded like something I would enjoy. Instead, being lost meant that you had no control, no sense of direction, but that's not the bad part. The bad part is that everyone else is heading to their destination. Everyone around you has all their shit figured out, and you're stuck in the abyss of helplessness. You're trapped with no room to breathe. You become lost in your own mind, restricted by your personal thoughts, and for what? Well, it is to find your path. Don't feel sad if you are lost, because being lost only means that there is a 100% chance that you will be found again. Don't be fooled by those who claim to know where they are going – they might be even more lost than you. You can change your outcome in life, and you can do it at your own pace.

Sometimes life moves too fast, slow it down for a bit, get lost, and then let something real in you to be found once again.

If you always know where you'll be, when

you'll be there, and how you will get there, then you skipped that day when you were on an elementry school sports team and they told you to have fun instead of just going out there and winning. Winning doesn't always mean happiness, and losing doesn't always mean sadness, it's how you play that determines our outcome. (Yes, of course I had to make a sports analogy for all those die-hard sports players. You're welcome).

Sometimes life goes too fast, so slow
it down for a bit and get lost.

60. Memories

There are many people that enter and then exit our lives. They come and go as they please, nothing is really permanent with them. The only sure thing is you; you and your memories. Those two things will always be in your life no matter what. Although not all memories are good, not everything in our life is smooth sailing. We will always encounter bumps in the road, but these things only make you wiser and stronger. Good or bad, it got you to the place you are today. Sort of like a chain reaction. If this certain event didn't happen, then this other thing wouldn't have happened. Even though the people that have existed in your life are gone physically, they are still there, mentally safe and sound in your memories. The good memories are what we hold onto the most. Whether it is looking at old pictures and thinking about when, where, and how it was taken. Or going somewhere that reminds you of a person you once knew and how they would enjoy it if they were still here. Anything can trigger a memory, even just the taste of food. You can even be in the shower (where most deep thinking occurs). Hold on to the warm and fuzzy ones, where you were so happy that nothing else in the world really mattered. It's unfortunate when the one person we didn't want to see disappear from our lives suddenly leaves. It was a chapter in your life, and now it has come to a close. They might show up again in later chapters, or they might not. The only thing you should remember is that the story continues. It doesn't stop for anyone or anything. Once you stop your story, your life becomes uninteresting and filled with remorse. Don't hang on to memorabilia that is in no way helping you to move forward with your life. Start fresh, and start clean, because a new chapter waits for no one. But to get your story started you need to be willing to open that book first.

The only thing you should remember
is that the story continues.

61. Motivational? I Think Not

Just to let you readers know this is not a motivational book. I'm not gonna tell you that you are no longer going to be fat if you just get up and exercise, because that's obvious. If you want a pick-me-up or a striking amount of motivation, give yourself a compliment. Cold, I know, but the world's cold (just preparing you). To be honest, motivation is slightly overrated. A million people probably disagree, but think about it. You really need someone or something to be able to do something? No, don't wanna do it? Then don't do it. Wanna do it? Then do it. It's That Simple. Yet I realize that this paragraph might sound motivational and uplifting, but, as I said before, this is not motivational. This is simply what life is. Thank you.

No, don't wanna do it? Then don't do it.
Wanna do it? Then do it.
It's that simple.

62. Music

The repeating patterns of noise that create songs that we listen to with our ears. We listen to fast-paced music when we are working out to pump us up. We listen to music when we want to lay down and hear soft, peaceful patterns of soulful rhythms filling our body with happiness. Some of us listen to music while doing homework/projects for school or work: this is focus music that pushes you to keep moving, and it can be a mixture of loud and soft songs depending on your taste. Music is another way to express ourselves. In movies, if the guy cannot talk to the girl because he is too nervous, then he will sing a song dedicated to her to tell her how he feels. People with similar tastes in music will somehow have a deeper connection with each other.

There is a powerful thing about music. It can drive our emotions in different directions just because we're listening to several beats with rhythms and patterns. Whether we are happy or sad, music is our outlet, our escape. We block out the rest of the world or have a wild party with all our friends. It brings people together or isolates us from irrelevant people. Whatever the reason, music never fails to impress.

Appreciate all music and stimulate your mind to go to your own place, your own world.

63. Off Topic

I'm not Holden Caulfield. (If you are not familiar with this reference, then I suggest you read Catcher in the Rye, it's a great novel about absolutely nothing, yet seems to be about everything.) Still, I am great at getting off-topic and trailing off into the unknown and the forgotten. You should definitely do this when you can. Maybe instead of staying on topic, you reflect on something that makes you think of another thing, and another, and so on, and on, and on forever, until someone tells you, "for the love of God, stop talking." Then it finally stops, but before then you could go on for days. I say go on and on for days, and if someone mutters the words stop, just walk away and carry on.

Allow yourself to be lost in random thoughts.

64. Originality

Sometimes we get caught up in following the pack. We go out for student body president, join a gazillion (yes, that's a real number) clubs, get those higher than high GPAs, and get really focused on college. For what? Yeah, yeah, standard living with job and money, security for the future. But what about happiness? We are all on the so-called conveyer belt to a standard life to please our parents. However, pleasing your parents shouldn't get in the way of finding yourself and your originality. Your originality is what sets you apart from everyone else. We are molded by our schools into a certain shape, made to obey certain things and go with certain trends, but sometimes we have to think outside of our proper tight-knit box. Nowadays it seems harder and harder to think for ourselves. So, just try not to be a broken record and discover yourself.

Discover yourself for you.

65. Our Imagination

I don't care how old you are; everyone has an imagination. Having said that, it's also clear that some people might have very little imagination, while others might have an excessive amount. Usually our dreams and fantasies are better than our current reality. I mean, who wants to face reality when your imagination will always be better? I know I don't. Except when I make my dreams/ fantasies a reality (yup, cheesy). Your imagination is just the outline or blueprint of what you can accomplish. If you dream it, you can achieve it (I think I saw that on a Nike shirt once). Everyone's dreams are different. We all want to accomplish something different in our life. Some want money, fame, help, time, etc. Me?

Well, I just want people to be happy.
Not just with themselves, but with each other.

I sure dream that one day everyone will be happy with each other. probably thinking ummm, whoever you are, that's stupid and most likely impossible. You're partly right, it's impossible, but not stupid. Just because I'm dreaming about it, I know for a fact that it will become a little bit more real. Don't worry, you didn't break my spirit. Let me tell you something, though. Everything is temporary. Emotions, money, even life is temporary. So, if you got a dream, you better go after that dream, or else someone else will, and you'll constantly wonder how your life would've changed if you had followed that dream. What's the damage? After all, it's all just temporary.

Dream something, dream anything,
and go after that dream.
You never know where it will lead you.

66. Out of Your Mind

There are times in our path where we are leading to an inevitable death; when our plates are full. We ave too many things to get done and not enough space to store it all. We need an escape. I have some suggestions. One thing that helps is exercise (eww, I know, but it is not as bad as it seems). This will help you get your mind off the things in your life that you don't want to deal with at this moment. Is it a good idea to ignore your problems? Absolutely not. But it does help your health to not let it overtake you, so that's a bonus. It will give you time to realx, calm down, and look at your problems from a different perspective. The second thing is sleep (yessssss, whooohoo). Sleeping, a seeming waste of a time, might be just what you need to cope with your current situation. Having enough rest can help you become more productive, and, as a plus, less cranky. Third thing would be to leave (yeah, that's dumb leave and go where?). Go anywhere, anywhere, but the place you are in right now. Getting away to a new location can help ease your mind. New scenery is very beneficial. Fourth and final thing is to breathe (mmm, as the in and out kind). You're thinking, forget to breath? How could I forget that? Well, as a yoga instructor once said, we remember to follow all the directions being given and focus on that so much, we forget to do the simplest of things, like breathing. Breathing deeply can naturally calm your body, giving you a better relief than popping a Xanax (a pill for "calming" down). If you are still stressed after all these things then... REPEAT.

Do not let your mind control you,
you control your mind.

67. Parents

We, as teenagers, find our parents to be a pain in our ass. Really, the only intention of the people I like to call oversized children who think they know everything is to protect and love you. Well, at least the intention of most parents is to protect and love you, that is. If that's not the case for you, I am deeply sorry, but there are always people out there who love you, and you might not even know it, so never forget that. The unfortunate part of unconditional love is that it's approached in all the wrong ways. Sometimes I feel that my parents aren't really acting like my parents. Like they're robots sent from the government to make sure I go to school, get good grades to get into college, get married, have children, and, hopefully, experience a short and painless death. Maybe that's a little dramatic, but that's the definition of teenager, so I might as well play the part.

No matter how nice you are to your parents, they will always interrogate you like a CSI agent trying to get valuable information out of you. The thing that they don't know is that the most exciting thing that happened during your day was that you got an extra cookie in your lunch box. They will lecture you till your ear falls off about not drinking and not smoking weed so much that you won't want to even hear the words come out of anyone's mouth. Then onto the next topic: they know what you're going through because they went to high school. The only key difference they forget to mention is that they went to high school a little over 30 years ago, and, if I'm not mistaken, a lot has changed since then according to my history book. However, if you'd like to prove me wrong, I can gladly show you the page number.

Many parents compare themselves to other parents or even to their own parents. They let you know that they're the "cool" parents. Overall, parents don't really know what they're talking about most of the time. On a few rare occasions they may have good advice about the world. After all, they have been in the "real" world. The point is, their intentions are pure, but they just have a hard time with the delivery. Try to remember that when they're talking to you; try to see the good intention part rather than the interrogation and ridicule. You will have plenty of fights, let me tell you, but eventually those fights have to end, and when peace finally comes, it's going to feel great. You will always be their child and that will never change, they will always be there for you.

I honestly think that when we are little, our parents are like angels. They are perfect and godlike, so we can't really relate to them. We don't realize our parents were kids too until later in life. We also find out later that our parents did stupid stuff as well. For me, that's when I truly connected to my parents. I realized they didn't belong on a pedestal, they were real! I felt the closest to them when I saw this. They were rebels! Actually my parents are still rebels, just in different ways.

I think we need to relate to our parents to understand them and respect their wishes. Sometimes, they do know best.

Note to parents:
Let us see the real you, who you
were and who you are.

68. Past. Present. Future.

Those three confusing concepts. People say: don't live in the past, but live in the present, so you can later enjoy the future (or something like that). And you know, I kind of agree. Do you? Although there are some conditions. I will try my best to forget the bad things about my past, but make sure to hold on to the good memories. And I will live in the present, but I will not forget how I made it here. And as for the future, whatever happens, well, happens. I don't have a schedule. Whatever comes at me, I guess I'll just go with it. I mean, what else can you do?

Learn from the past,
live in the present,
be excited about the future.

69. Peace

Many people seek peace in their life. It might be through meditation, quiet time, family time, friend time, etc. Even countries seek peace through treaties with other countries. In France, there is the Eiffel tower. There are pillars in front of it. Most people disregard these columns, since there is a gigantic piece of art in front of them. Each column has scripts in a different language. They represent countries that France made peace with. It is an underappreciated beauty. To find peace, you need balance. Take on the role of the ying-yang. We can't have good without the bad, and we can't have darkness without light. Even if there is turmoil, tranquility will come soon. Peace of mind involves putting negative things out of your mind.

Maybe others have ongoing conflicts, and you are just caught in the crossfire, so you need to brush off that conflict. Don't stay mad. It helps no one. Actually, stress that comes from anger is hurting you, because it can even physically shrink your brain. So for your well-being and the well-being of others, stay cool as a cucumber.

Don't stay mad.
It doesn't help anyone.

70. Personal Dance Party

At times we can feel a little gloomy. We are stuck between that emotion that is plain old sad to down right depressed. At this moment I believe there is only one thing to do. YES! You are exactly right! Have an individual dance party. Isn't that what you were thinking? Well, a personal dance party might sound unappealing, but don't be so quick to dismiss it. Just think that when we go to parties, we most likely dance with our friends/family. That gives us a good feeling, right? For some, yes, this act is quite enjoyable, and it's not some pity party, but a pick-me-up just for you. So, why not copy this off the people who do it (like me) and dance the gloominess away? Try it. My parents always told me that you should try everything once, then if you don't like it, you don't have to do it again, but if some miracle occurs where you love it, then you'll be so happy that you did it. Sooooooo, put on any song that you fancy and dance away! No one's watching, it's just you, so dance to your heart's content and then eat whatever you like after, because you just earned yourself a lot of free calories, my friend.

A personal dance party might sound unappealing, but don't be so quick to dismiss it.

71. Politics and The News

What is politics? Well, the dictionary version is: the activities of governments concerning the political relations between countries. Seems simple. Except if we add a little reality to that sentence, we get this: high authority officials or presidents of countries fighting (verbally or physically) over unnecessary things that most likely belong to someone from an entirely different country. Basically, the governments never went to kindergarten to learn how to share.

Although politics waste the government's time and money, something that doesn't waste time is the news. I watch the news every day (or at least read it) when I wake up in the morning, and I'm only 17 years old. You should always know about events taking place in the world you live in. Whether what's happening is good or bad, it will help you understand the atmosphere you are currently a part of. The news' sole purpose is to state the facts straight to your face. No bullshit. Well, at least that would be the idea.

The government never went to kindergarten to learn how to share.

72. Rainy Days

The sky is gray and gloomy. Light drizzles mixed with spontaneous downpours throughout the day. The sidewalks become wet along with your clothes. You look out the window, immediately wanting to curl up in your bed and watch Netflix or put your headphones on and tune out the world.

Some people like thunderstorms, some hate them. Whichever category you fall into, we all seem to feel different on a rainy day. I like the rain. It always makes me ponder life.

I think we should let the rain
into our lives and get wet.
That is what I feel about rain.

73. Reading Between the Lines

Everything we read, watch, or hear has a backstory. There is always a story inside a story. All the movies you watch have a storyline, and it has a hidden deeper message. Whether it is to value family, to hang on to the love you see in the movies because sometimes it happens in real life, to appreciate war veterans and what they do for our country, to believe in conspiracy theories or ghost stories (could they be real? Probably not... maybe though, who knows), or enjoy a magical fantasy land that proves magic is what always kept us young at heart, to laugh at some stupid humour (that most likely doesn't have a backstory but is funny as hell, so who cares), and much more. Movies are not made just for the heck of it. Every director always wants to tell a story, a true story that will get into the person's head and stay there for as long as it can. Writers will most likely tell you the real shit that you can't identify in the movies. They give you the details, so that you can better understand a concept and create in your head pictures of certain characters. Reading between the lines plastered in your face can sometimes be tricky, but identifying the underlying story is a very smart skill. Look at that, you're a brainiac, and you didn't even know it. In this book there is no reading between the lines. I am telling you everything straight from my own cluttered mind. There is no backstory. Because, frankly, I am sick of people pretending that everything is good on the outside, but on the inside there is a massive disaster. I feel that it's time for everyone to put their genuine thoughts on a page, on the lines, in front of one's face. What people do with them is their choice, but at least your words are out there with no confusion.

So, I suggest if you make a movie, write a book, give a speech, or even simply talking to someone, say what you need to say. Leave everything out on the table, or the chair, or the counter (haha, get it), and don't look back.

Stop making people guess what you are truly feeling and thinking.

74. Relationships

Oh, relationships. They are complicated, messy, fun, happy, sad, annoying, etc. Eventually everyone will be in one or in many, for some of you.

Rule #1 of dating: you have to be friends with the other person first. Establish a good base, as most relationships that the girl and boy, boy and boy, girl and girl, or even they and them are in, involve best friends. Although if you are 40 and alone, with your parents telling you to get married, well, be my guest and go on match.com, because you don't have many of your best years left ;). But if you are better off alone, and you are honestly OK with it, then so be it. It's not necessarily normal to get married and have children, people of today's society have just made it that way. I think there is no real right and wrong in relationships, just you and your feelings, which are anything but crystal clear. You just need to do the thing that makes you happy.

The definition of relationship is a messy love fest, so it's never perfect.

75. Run Your Own Race

This title, my fellow homosapiens, is a phrase, a figure of speech, if you will. It pertains to only one person. Yourself. You. An individual person; you get the idea. Sometimes we forget that in life not everything is a competition. Sure, a little healthy competition is good once in a while, but it shouldn't consume you. Being the only one on top can get a little lonely. It's a rush at first, but if it's the only thing you think about, it no longer is enjoyable. While we are "running" this "race" called our life, we shall not think about it from the perspective of others. The only thing that matter is our progress; if we are becoming better and happier everyday, then we have already won the race. Bettering yourself doesn't have to come at the cost of another person. Everyone has a purpose to fill, so go out, win your race, and you will become more and more satisfied with what you see when you look in the mirror.

If we are becoming better and happier every day,
then we have already won the race.

76. Save The Trees

Every day in our schools and workplaces we are encouraged to recycle, because somehow this act of recycling our water bottles makes us feel like we are saving the planet. Don't get me wrong, everyone who recycles should be very proud of themselves. However, we can do more. Right now we are destroying our Earth. All the pollution, cutting down trees (our main source of oxygen, I might add), and overall wasting of things that we take for granted every day. We are killing our animals, making our air toxic, and not thinking about the overall consequences. Don't you want the future generation to enjoy the things you did as a kid? Are we so selfish that we would want to deprive them of going to the zoo, camping in the large forests, or even having clean drinking water? We are given money to cut down trees in order to make more money that can be given to cut down more trees. And we will keep doing this until we have nothing left. Does that make any sense even remotely? No. No worries, my friends, there can be a change. There can be an adjustment that will allow us to stay on Earth, and not have to be shipped off to an unknown planet that may or may not be entirely safe (Earth 2.0). Next time you write on paper use both sides, take a faster shower, recycle those bottles; just little things that can have a big impact. Then you can say you had a part in saving the planet. I mean, I'd put that on my resume. Including being the 2008 person of the year in Time Magazine (again, in 2008 the magazine made everyone their person of the year). Don't be mean. Go Green!!!

Little things add up.
Next time you write on paper, use both sides.

77. Scary

What's your worst fear? Haunted houses, spiders, snakes, people, public speaking, ducks, clowns? Everyone has a horrible fear, no matter what it is, everyone knows what they are afraid of. You have heard people say they have or have wanted to overcome their fear. If you are truly afraid of something, it is quite hard to overcome it. Eventually, later in your life, you may overcome that obstacle in your life or it might be an unnecessary fear to overcome because you can just move around it, Whatever works for you. If you are thinking about some of your biggest fears right now, think of the ones that could benefit you in the future if you work through them. Got one in mind? Okay, now simply just start the process of overcoming it. Cross it off the bucket list and make it an experience you'll never forget. Being afraid is normal, it doesn't make you a coward. The bravest people I know are often the ones scared the most.

Fear shouldn't stop you from doing what you love.

78. Season Agenda

What the hell is a season agenda? Glad you asked, my friend. Oh, it's just something I invented using my unpredictable and improbable imagination. You're welcome... ha. ha. ha. Okay, so I guess I should explain it, because you guys aren't mind readers or anything.

- *Summer* (sun): Get sunglasses or a hat and a music device with headphones. Go outside. Look at the grass and admire it. Run to the grass. Sit on the grass, wait two seconds, look around. Proceed to lay down and look up at the sky. Embrace the sun and get some vitamin D. Smell the freshly cut grass as it tickles your exposed skin. Lay out there for a second just listening to what nature has to offer you. Then go on to pick your favorite chill song (a.k.a., favorite song) and listen to it with no interruptions, just being with no one but yourself.

- *Fall* (rain): Get a rain jacket, rain boots, and, possibly, a musical device with headphones if you can keep it from getting wet. Go outside. Make sure it's pouring (or that there is at least a heavy drizzle). Step out in the open. It can be anywhere, but you must be alone. Don't worry if your hair or clothes get drenched in the rain, because that can dry. Once you are out, open your mouth and let the rain drops inside. Taste good? Then find the biggest puddle you can find. No wimpy shit. I want the biggest puddle, man, don't disappoint. And...1-2-3... jump!! (straight into the puddle if you didn't catch that, lol). Now that you are drenched, just walk, run, or do whatever you want to do for however long you feel is necessary.

- *Winter* (snow): Last but certainly not least, the magical winter wonderland that is snow. Grab your wintertime coat, gloves, hat, snow pants, etc. Go outside. Smell that winter air. It's fresh and crisp. Everything is frozen into one large icicle. Now go jump into the fluffy white stuff we call snow. Lay down, and make a snow angel! Yes, that thing you used to do or still do when those winter months come along. Once you've got a kickass angel, it's time to make... a snowman! (At this point if you are not thoroughly satisfied and enjoying yourself, then go inside, but I highly doubt that will happen). Put your headphones in, play that Christmas music (or that one song that is stuck in your head), and start building. When you are finished, come back and read the rest. Well, how'd that feel? You feel like a little kid again? Good. That was the point. Alright, what's being a kid if not having some hot chocolate? Go inside, have a cup or six, cozy up in a blanket, and sit by the fire. After constant movement comes extensive rest.

Experience every season with your inner child.
Remember to play in this life.

79. Secrets

Everyone has had their fair share of secrets. You are most likely keeping at least one secret or, even more likely, many. Our world runs on secrets. Everyone has a secret, because whether it's a dark one or not so dark one, it's still a secret. The thing about secrets is that they will always find a way of coming out, no matter how hard you try to keep it to yourself, even if you take it all the way to your grave. Nobody is entirely open with everyone, because opening up to people is very scary. You don't have to open up to people if you don't want to, it's not a law. Although people are very nosy, it's not your job to fuel their curiosity with dirty secrets; especially if it's not your secret to tell. However, there is a difference between a good secret and a bad secret.

Do not carry too much weight on the inside.
Let things go.

80. Shower Time

The constant struggle of not wanting to get into the shower, but once you're in, you never want to get out. Shower time is a constant in all our days, day or night, a way to become clean. We wash away all the crap that we have collected throughout the day, whether it is physical or mental crap that we've carried around. Some of us, secretly all of us, use this time to think deeply. We feel like actors in a famous movie, having deep thoughts about our life, submerged in our mind. We might be thinking about the happy memories or we might cry since no one can see us behind that protective shower curtain.

It's just our time. Our true alone time.
Take the time to have a nice
conversation with yourself.

81. Siblings

Siblings are kind of weird. One minute you want to kill them, the next you are singing a duet to a popular song and laughing uncontrollably. They annoy you, make you angry, and are overall a pain in the ass. They might even be annoying you while you are reading this. But remember you are family and that if anyone tries to hurt or make your brother/sister feel bad, you need to defend them. Make that bitch scared. Make sure that he/she never messes with your sibling again. They have no right. You have the right, because you are family, and most of the time you're kidding. That bully doesn't know what they're talking about, so smack them down. No blood or black eyes though ;)

Always take care of your sibling.
They are the most precious gift.

82. Sick Days

Tissues, cough and cold medicine, cough drops, hot tea, and body aches. We have all been sick. It's not a fun thing to be. You almost feel like that flu shot you got 3 months in advance hardly worked. Sometimes I feel that a day feeling crappy in bed is a day wasted. Why do we get sick? I don't know, that is for those complex thinkers out there to discover. But when you are sick, there are usually people to take care of you. It feels nice to be taken care of. I guess in those few days to a week that you feel crappy, there is someone there for you that makes you feel better both mentally and physically. If you do not have someone to take care of you, well, then you have to take care of yourself (wow, way to go me for pointing out the obvious), but honestly you have to. You have to cheer yourself up, which is not an easy thing to do, but I know you can do it. Cheering yourself up will take that sickness away. Also do not be one of those people who are in denial that they are sick, because you are just going to make people around you sick, which is not a good way to make friends, so if you are sick, feel better and cheer up. ;) Make time for the people who matter to you, especially if they are sick.

If we are always too busy for the important people in our lives when they just need a little cheering up or a simple hello, we are doing something seriously wrong in our lives.

83. Slowing Down

Stop!!! Whatever you are doing, drop it. Stop it. And don't start again until you've read this whole thing. Okay, now that I have your full attention I want to share something very important. Most human beings on our planet are very busy all the damn time!!! They've got no room to breathe or pee. I mean, some people need to chill out. Take a chill pill, my dad would always say. Some of us want the time to go by fast when we are waiting for school to get out or waiting to get out of our painful jobs that we just can't handle anymore. But if we really value our life, we should savor those moments. Just take a deep breath. Go, do it now. The 4-7-8 rule. Breathe in for 4 seconds, hold it for 7, and breathe out for 8. Do it a couple of times until you feel calm. Feel better yet? I know I do. Look around you and take it all in. Take in all your surroundings and never forget who you are. You see, in all the hustle, fast pace, our forever moving forward life, we get caught up. So, don't get caught up any longer.

Savor every moment like it's your last,
and one day you'll be right!

84. Small Talk

This is the sort of talk that you use when you are on a first date, talking to someone that you barely know, or avoiding the main idea that you know that specific person is not gonna like. It really is just a distraction from the main topic. It's the death of a good conversation:

Hey!
Hey, how are you?
Good. You?
Fine, thanks.
So what do you do for a living?
Oh, I'm a (fill in the blank), you?
And so on and so on and so on...

Please for the love of god, or the universe, or whatever, don't be this person. Cut out the bull-shit. Things will go much smoother, be much more interesting, and turn out way, way, wayyyyyyyyy less boring. I mean, come on, nobody really cares what your favorite color is or what you like to do in your free time. I mean, sure, you can say these things in a relationship, where people actually care. But if not, use one of my favorite sayings: "Cut – The – Bullshit», por favor.

Do yourself a favour and be real, it's a time saver.

85. Society

Oh, well, what can I say about our socicty today. I can tell you one thing. We are different nowadays. This generation of teenagers and young adults are much more accepting than before. History is a constant pattern of the same issues consisting of different events. There was a time when people were against African Americans. People could not even stand the sight of them. Today we know this as a dark and sick hatred. In the 21st century we have a constant problem with homophobia. It keeps coming up. Once we get over people being homophobic, aliens will invade Earth and we will become "Alien Phobic". And the cycle will continue forever. Criticizing people for who they are. That's the specialty of the people of this world. We will tell you to be yourself, but when you become your true self people criticize you because you're not "good enough". That's crap, come on, you're better than that. Honestly, nobody asked you for your opinion. Remember I said you're entitled to your opinion, but using your opinion to make someone feel bad about themselves is not okay. You might be thinking, who am I to tell you what to think? You are absolutely correct, I have no right, but has anyone ever told you to think before you speak? Yeah, well, think about how all the different ways you use your words can affect the people around you next time you say something.

Using your opinion to make someone feel bad about themselves is not okay.

86. Speeches

Martin Luther King Jr. and Hitler are actually quite similar. You might be questioning my intelligence after just reading that sentence, but I promise I have a good reason. They both used to practice their speeches in front of a mirror to make sure they could get their message across to the group of people that looked up to them for guidance. Some people are nervous to give speeches. Mostly because they fear what people might think of it. Imagining everyone in their underwear is one way to get over the fear. But there is another thing that will cure the fear for a long time. Ready?

Stop caring what strangers think!!!

Gosh, people care so much about what they will look like and how they will sound to others that they forget to think and be themselves. Forget everyone else. If you don't care (and I mean truly don't care what people think), then you will be your most confident self. If you honestly don't give a shit, nothing can stop you. Your speech will be more true and honest. So, don't give a shit what people think, do, or say, just live the best way you can.

Not caring about the judgments of strangers is not the same as not caring. It's not the same as not caring about the people. It's not the same as not caring what the important people in your life say or think. The people who truly matter don't judge, but they want to help you live the life you want to live. They keep us accountable and keep us on our path. You need to care about what you say, about standing by your ideas, being passionate about what matters to you –

not about what strangers or society say.

Stop caring what people think!!!
The people who truly matter don't judge.

87. Spread the Positivity

Positivity is like a disease. It's contagious. It is a proven fact that the people around you alter your current mood. If there are elated people around you, your mood is guaranteed to be slightly more if not much more joyful. Same thing with negativity – your mood will change within a second. Negativity is spread around too often. More and more children are becoming cynical of their futures, and it's just not healthy. When we are young, we are full of dreams and possibilities. Once we get older, our dreams shouldn't stop. You're never too old to achieve happiness. So do yourself and everyone around you a favor and spread the delight of a smile to someone who looks down. For all you know, you could turn their whole day around.

When we are young,
we are full of dreams and possibilities.
Once we get older, our dreams shouldn't stop.

88. Strength

Strength is not determined by how big your muscles are or by how much you can bench press. Strength is something different. It is a reaction that occurs when you've lost something. Whether it is something material or something mental, you have lost it. You don't know what to do, you're just angry. You're angry at God, or the world, or yourself. Everything just sucks for you right now. Okay, so you're lower than low. Now what? Well, now all eyes are on you, considering what you are gonna do about it. Are you gonna mope around and complain about your sucky life, because of this one thing that sent you all the way down? Or are you gonna get up and do something about it? This is all determined by how much strength you have. Just moving on, starting fresh, sucking it up, and making the best of what you have. Make do with what you have and don't rely on anyone to just feed you things from the tip of a shiny silver spoon, because that won't happen. Your life is all you. So, if you're sitting down anxious and determining your next move, GET UP. Get up and do this exercise I call The Superman.

1. Stand up
2. Put your hands on your hips

3 Spread your feet and shoulders
4 Arch back
5 Put your head up
6 Repeat the words "I can do this"
7 Stand there for however long you think is necessary in order to believe this statement

Stand proud. Very few people nowadays gets approval from their loved ones. However, it doesn't matter if everyone's against you; I am with you and I am proud.

Your life is all you.

89. Strength Of A Woman

We live in a time of achievement, results, ego, always chasing the next best thing; yet being blind to the beauty that is right in front of us.

Media teaches us to put more worth in how we look and how we dress; where showing your skin has more value and wirht then showing your true inside, your vulnerability.

A message to all my lovely women in the world.

I know we are more independent and have found the courage to chase our own dreams and aspirations. But we aware, that in doing so we either become strong women or women of strength.

Strong Women vs. Women of Strength

A strong woman works out every day to keep her body in shape.
A woman of strength builds relationships to keep her soul in shape.

A strong woman is not afraid of anything.
A woman of strength shows courage in the midst of fear.

A strong woman would not let anyone get the best of her.
A woman of strength gives the best of herself to everyone.

A strong woman makes mistakes and avoids the same in the future.
A woman of strength realizes life's mistakes can also be unexpected blessings and capitalizes on them.

A strong woman wears a look of confidence on her face.
A woman of strength wears grace.

A strong woman has faith that she is strong enough for the journey.

A woman of strength has faith that it is in the journey that she will become strong.

Never lose sight of your inner strength.

90. Summer

Those short three months of bliss you feel when there is the scorching sun on your face, and you have time to waste. It feels so good. To just take a break and relax. Swim, play outside, go to camps (some sadly still have to go to work), have sleepovers, go to parties, read, watch Netflix, whatever you do, you are free. You are happy.

So don't waste these summers,
because you only have so many in your lifetime.

91. Take A Walk

Our lives have a way of taking a toll not only on our bodies, but on our minds as well. We feel tired mentally and physically. Sometimes we just need a break from our lives and especially from the people in them. Remember, it's not life itself that is complicated, but the people that are in our life that we allow to make it that way, so choose your companions and acquaintances wisely. The best way to clear your mind is to just take a walk. Yup, I know. Who knew it was that easy? Put your headphones in your ears and play your favorite song on repeat while you walk and reminisce about absolutely nothing; be free like a bird who just got the hang of their wings for the first time. This will allow you to become more open, less flustered, and to get out of that crowded corner. After all: "nobody puts baby in the corner!" Hopefully you know what movie that's from; if you don't, ask someone immediately and watch the damn movie.

Most members of this generation are constantly on their (our) phones. I mean, we've all heard our parents say: "You're always on your phone", "You never interact with others". We've all heard this. So, rest your eyes and make your parents happy, for once, and go for a walk. (Wait, you mean go outside and exercise, like get fresh air?). Yes, go outside, trust me, it will be good for your soul, and you won't be as tired.

A walk can help in so many ways. It can help us cool down when we get too heated up. Not necessarily in terms of temperature, but in relation to our state of mind, getting too sad or too mad, filled with emotion. If you feel like that, take a walk. It's guaranteed to help.

Now close this book and play outside. (Play outside? I haven't done that since I was in elementary school) Yeah, remember how happy you used to be in elementary school? You want that feeling again? Then go play and don't pick this book up again until you are as happy as you were when it was just normal to play outside. Adios.

Be free like a bird who just spread their wings for the first time.

92. Take Time Off

We work hard all day and all night. Whether we do it at our jobs or in school, there is time and effort put into every day (for most of us). However, after all this effort we need a break. No one can work forever. There needs to be some time left to relax. It's good for the brain to take a day off. Sometimes we tend to get caught up in our work. We get flustered with the current state we put ourselves in. That's the moment you know to step back. Take a nap (something you probably haven't done since kindergarten nap time). Rejuvenate yourself. Go out with friends or family and have a good time. They also need a break. When you are done, go back to your work with fresh eyes. Don't work too hard, but don't become a lazy ass. Find a balance between work and play. We get caught up in our work or in our laziness, and never get to the point. Well, taking small breaks will help you enjoy your work more, but you need to keep a balance. When I was writing this, I definitely needed more than a few breaks here and there. A happy medium will put a grin on that face of yours.

Find a balance between work and play.

93. Teachers

You may have heard that common quote associated with teachers. If you haven't, well, here it is: "Those who can do, do, and those who can't, teach." A very cruel quote, if you think about it. Teachers, most of the time, are people who want to help you and encourage you to learn. Even though some of them have lost sight of why they became teachers to begin with, they are definitely not doing it for the money...They are literally teaching the future of the world. That is a pretty hard job to do. You should always become friends with your teachers and cut them some slack. Most of them work very hard and receive the shittiest recognition. Some teachers are easier to get along with than others, but as long as you have made the effort, you're doing the right thing. Treating your teacher with respect is something they will never forget.

Note to Teacher:
Remember how much impact your
words and kindness have on us.

94. Teenagers

All righty, this one is actually for the adults, believe it or not. Listen. Kids, tweens, teenagers, whatever, most of us are harmless. I'm really in no place to talk about parenting. I mean, your teenager might be the popular party type. If so, stop reading this and start scolding. If not? Keep reading, of course. We are destined for screw-ups beyond compare, but most of us will pick up the pieces at the end, get up, turn around, and keep moving forward. They teach us in school to learn, so that we won't make mistakes. Although they're forgetting that in life you are gonna make mistakes in order to learn from them. Anyway, most of us are harmless. To be fair, we make a lot, a lot, a lot, of stupid, stupid decisions (yes, repeating a word more than once creates emphasis). Even though at times we can be extremely dumb, you gotta cut us some slack. Our prefrontal cortex (the thing in your head that controls your impulsive decisions) is not even fully developed! So really, you can't blame us. Okay? Okay, but in all seriousness, being a teenager is the hardest chapter in one's life. It's filled with pressure, hormones, and crowds of people in a cramped place. I mean, ew, it does not sound appetizing at all. Kill me now, I'm a teenager. No one says "Oh boy, do I just love being a teenager", it's unheard of. We are trying to figure it out ourselves, while going through pressures of knowing what we are going to do for the rest of our lives, and, my god, it's entirely too much. When does the anarchy stop!? Alright, a little melodramatic, but what do I care? If I want to be melodramatic, I will. And you should too, if you want to! :)

Being a teenager is the hardest chapter in one's life.
Please take the time to listen to
us, talk to us, support us...
That's really not too much to ask.

95. Thanksgiving

Ahhh, yesss, a day of food and overall happiness (because you are consuming large amounts of food while being surrounded by friends and family). What could be better?! The answer is nothing. Nothing is better than that. Enjoy the family time and think about things that you are grateful for. Here is a list of some things you may not think you should be thankful for: Be thankful for...

The taxes you pay, because it means that you are still employed.

The clothes that fit a little too tight, because it means you have enough to eat.

The shadow that watches you, because it means that you are out in the sunshine.

A lawn that has been mowed, windows that have been washed, and gutters that have been cleaned because that means you have a home.

The spot you find at the far end of the parking lot, because it means you have the capability to walk.

All the complaining you hear about the government, because it means we have freedom of speech.

The lady behind you in church who sings off-key, because it means that you can hear.

The huge pile of laundry and ironing to be done, because it means your loved ones are nearby.

Finally, the alarm that goes off in the early morning hours, because it means that you are alive.

It's all about perspective,
How are you looking at things around you?

96. The Big Life Plan

What is the point of life when life itself has no point? That's just it. There are no blueprints that map out the life you will have or the encounters you'll deal with throughout your journey on this earth. There is only you, and there's everything that makes you happy. Never let go of happiness, because when happiness is gone there is nothing left to live for. Even if all your happiness comes from a distant memory, hold on to it, and never let it go.

Make your big life plan, but be ready to change it when you know your heart is leading you somewhere else.

97. The One And Only Passion

Everyone has at least one thing in their life they are passionate about. It could be a sport, a club, a certain subject, an instrument, or an extracurricular activity. Whatever it may be, most of the passions that we have we are good at and tend to pursue most of our time in that certain thing. Some people have had this passion in life since the day they were born. Others have some trouble figuring out what they love. I, for one, do not have a passion for anything, yet. I seem to like everything an equal amount. Nothing in my life stands out to me. Although, as I said before, some people find their passion much later in life. And that is okay!

Your time will come eventually, I promise.
I am waiting right there with you.

98. Traveling

One thing that is on everyone's or most people's bucket lists is to travel the world. To explore the unknown territory, to have a great time doing it. With friends, family, or alone. Whether is cliff-diving, or backpacking, or doing whatever makes you happy. So, travel the world and have fun, document it on social media (or don't), whatever you do, just make sure your having fun.

Stop thinking and talking about
it, just go and do it.

99. TV Shows

Ahh, TV... Let me tell you it is great. It is the only acceptable way to be brainwashed by actors and actresses acting out stories that people have created from their own imagination. No matter how busy I am, I always find time for TV. It is something of a way of life for the majority of the current population. Yeah, it is probably a waste of time that I could spend changing the world or whatever. But some people don't understand some of the very valuable lessons that I have learned from quality television. Unfortunately, dramatic reality TV has taken over the minds of people across the world, although I have to admit they can be addicting. It is also very relaxing, and sometimes we need to have a break and relax. We need to sink our minds into a made-up storyline with drama, or humor, or thrillers, or even the occasional documentary.

In a weird way, those shows alter our views of the world and make us think about things we wouldn't normally think about. They get us attached to something that isn't real, but at the same time feels real to us. They make us laugh and cry, but, most importantly, bond with others who enjoy the same things we do. So, next time your mom or dad say that television is a waste of time, remind them that without TV you won't be able to learn new things on a deeper level, and it would be a shame to keep you from learning. Wouldn't it?

T.V. is not bad, it is what you choose to watch that can be a waste of time or a learning experience.

100. You're Never Fully Dressed Without a Smile

How you start your day sets the tone for the rest of it. If you wake up on the wrong side of the bed, as they say, and put yourself into a dark mood, the whole day is ruined. However, simply using your smiling muscles, even if you are not happy, sends a trigger message to your brain and produces happiness chemicals. As you can see, I am very scientific and totally know what I am talking about (said in sarcastic tone). It doesn't matter, because what I am saying is 100% true. Whether it's because of these chemicals or whatever, you will feel better. As for being fully dressed... Your outfit is great, your hair is glossy, and your shoes match the color scheme of the whole ensemble. What are you missing? You guessed it. A smile. That's pretty much it. There is nothing else to say, because it's self-explanatory, and I am sure you are a pretty smart person. So, hopefully, this wasn't a huge waste of your time. Until the next entry, adios.

Using your smiling muscles,
even if you are not happy,
sends a trigger message to your brain
and produces happiness chemicals.

101. Your Birthday

Every year you get one year older than the last. It seems like a regular annual thing, yet we make quite a big deal about it sometimes. Especially if you are turning 16, 18, 21, 30, 40, 50, or 100. Some people like their birthday so much, they classify it as a part of a birthday week or even a birthday month. As if everyone else's birthday that same week or month was irrelevant. Seems selfish when you put it that way, but it is somewhat true. Others despise their birthday. Mostly if you are older and do not want to get old. But we cannot be young forever. My grandmother just turned 69, and she still loves her birthday. She does not care that she's getting older. After all, age is just a number. And everyone else is simply content with it. They do not like to make a big deal about it, but still acknowledge that they are getting older instead of hiding it or flaunting it around and telling everyone they randomly meet. So, next time you have your birthday feel happy and content. Do not go crazily overboard and put all the attention on yourself. On the other hand, do not lie about your age and hide the fact that you are getting older. Besides if you're not getting older, then you are dead, my friend, and we would not want that now would we?

Celebrate your birthday by making a
difference in someone else's life.
It will be the greatest gift you will receive.

102. Valentine's Day

Love is in the air, and you are either in love or disgusted with all the couples that are in love. Those are the two types of people you will encounter on the "hearts" day.

You might be in a new or old relationship doing fun things with your partner. Or you could be a bitter single sitting on your couch, watching sappy movies with a tub of ice cream and one large spoon, wishing you had someone in your life. Unfortunately, there is no in-between. But if you happen to be one of those in-between people, then well you are just one of the special lucky ones. What's important is to focus on the good in the people around us. They will have their flaws, but they will help us create meaningful relationships.

Treat your loved ones like it is
Valentine's Day every day.

Helpful Tips to lead a Happier/Minimalist/More Satisfying Life

01. Be Generous!: There are countless benefits to being generous. That feeling you get when you see another person smile because of an act of kindness you have done is like no other feeling on earth. I do not mean just getting out your checkbooks and calling it good. I mean simply brightening someone's day. Simply giving a compliment. Giving a random hug to someone, just because you can.

02. Embrace the Gratitude: Make a list of all the things that you are grateful for, and if it is a long one, then kiss it because you are blessed. Once you realize that you have it pretty good, you will begin to realize that others around you can definitely be helped. This will help you open your heart.

"You can never have too much gratitude.
A simple thank you can have a domino effect because...
Gratitude sets the attitude
Attitude sets the atmosphere
Atmosphere creates the environment
And The environment changes the world"

03. Find a person you believe in: Find someone that you see has a potential for success or even something greater. Invest your time in someone who is passionate about a certain thing and watch as they blossom. Talk to them, become friends, go to parties and all-night ragers, or whatever you feel is necessary to do. Do not worry about wasting your time, because time is meant to be wasted. Why do you think we have so much of it? (Average lifespan is 657,450 hours just for your information, and that is plenty of time to waste.)

04. Live a more minimalist life: We are constantly getting sucked into the commercial aspects of life. Dragging ourselves through small talk and useless conversation. Talking to ourselves because we feel a gaping void of emptiness. Something is missing. Material things will make me happy, but only for a split second that is gone in the blink of an eye. Is that what I want? A life of nothingness? A life filled with so little love that the only thing that can fix my broken heart is a coffee cup with a signature Starbucks logo on it? No. I refuse to accept it. I refuse to give in to the state of normalcy that keeps me constantly exhausted and to live almost a century with no thrill or excitement. All I really need is food, water, fresh air, and a humble place to call home. A minimalist life is a life less traveled by most, because it is an existence that lacks security and stability. But they are very much mistaken. For, you see, the life that is less traveled is a concept that we do not yet fully understand. However, have you heard any complaints from the people who lead this life?

Looks like we have some re-evaluating to do.
Just a thought. :)

The End Of the Rainbow

Wow, we are getting close to the end here. Oh, what to say. Hmmmm... trying to think of something inspirational to send you off feeling good. I'll tell you a few things.

You are pretty damn cool for listening to me, or, should I say, for reading about what I have to say about the world. Never thought someone would want to. Sometimes you're going to be mad, sad, angry, or often cynical about the world around you. But don't let it overcome you. It's okay to be depressed and feel like your whole world is falling through your fingertips. I know what depression feels like and trust me - it's hell on earth. But you'll learn to get over it (and not in the way where people don't believe in mental illnesses way. The way where you learn to love not only someone else, but yourself as well). You're brave and tremendously strong for making it this far in the world. Wonder how far you will go? Well, only one way to find out! (That was pretty inspirational if I do say so myself).

Now I'm really done. Here comes an end to my endless rambling about random things in life. Yes, you may applaud if you need, but it's totally unnecessary (she says in sarcastic tone).

I have told you about my journey, my thoughts, curiosities, etc., and you have patiently listened. However, the wondering never stops, so it is now your turn to branch out and question the ramifications of life. This is the end. There is nothing else for me to do or say. My hope is that you feel a sense of relief that you are not the only one who is weird and crazy. I am weird and crazy! And even though I have no idea who I am, where I am, or what I am doing with my existence... it doesn't matter! Well, it shouldn't matter anyway, because we are all human beings, and human beings are all cool crazy weirdos which you should embrace and learn to love. Don't let those people that say they know who they are and where they are going bring you down...as most of them really do not know either. Do better. Be better. Be who you are, love what you do, make mistakes, laugh, cry, get excruciatingly mad, throw chairs, get the flu, hug a stranger, eat till your stuffed, win, lose, sleep, party, tell someone that they are important to you, and love them for forever.

Do what ever makes you happy,
because you only have one shot at life. So don't waste it.

In the end all these things may just sound simple and self-explanatory. However, you would be surprised how many people lack common human decency. With the purest of intentions, I give you this little book to look through just in case you forget to be the kind of people I know all of you are.

Now what are you still doing here reading this book? Leave. Give this book to someone who needs it and go! Get out! Get out and go live!

Love,

Rainbow (Natasha Chinoy)

Good Luck!!!

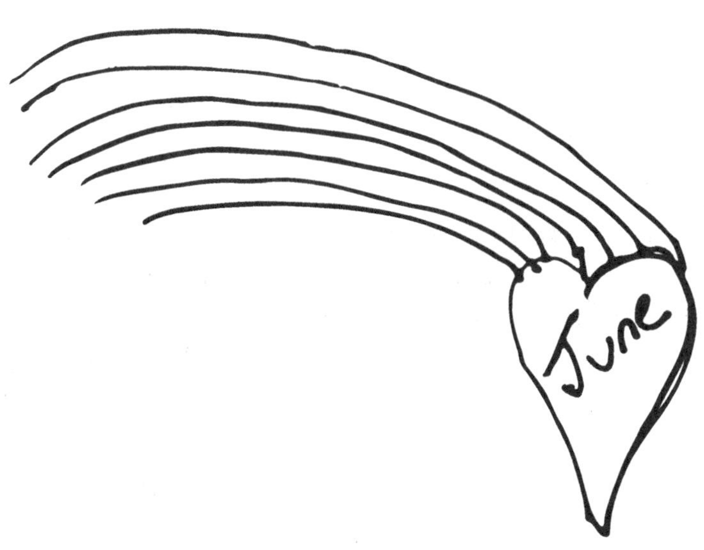

About Myself

Me... A weird thing to think about...

One way to get to know yourself is asking others what they think of you. Specifically, your close family and friends. These are the people that might see things in you that you have not seen as yet - the real you. However, do they really know you? Our true selves have a ying and a yang, a good part and a bad part, that we might not want to let other people see. The co-existence between the two, the balance between them fills our soul. Still, some of us have too much of ying or a yang. When this happens, one aspect overcomes the other, and our self is out of balance, so we might not be seen by others as we truly are, because we are caught in one aspect of ourselves. (Have you caught on yet that I do not like talking about myself).

Also, some people, even close people, might not see everything we are, because we show a different picture of ourselves when we are alone than when we are with someone. Despite this, in rare occasions we act with true sincerity and we see others express this true sincerity as well. Those people who can be honest and genuine and can allow us to see the real person rather than a pretentious wannabe, bringing out our own sincerity, should be cherished. Never lose sight of those people.

What makes the real you? Your personality, capabilities, and/or thoughts on various topics. So, how do I know who I am? Well, I don't. However, I do know that I strive to be the best version of myself, whatever that may entail. This is a tricky thing, you see. I could say I am a good friend, a caring person, and that I have a passion to find my passion. But this is what everyone could say. We are all trying to be individuals, but what we don't realize is that the way we perceive ourselves is based off of the individuals that are around us every day. We try to be unique, but in reality we are all slowly conforming to be the same way.

If I have to talk about myself and who I am;
well, then I am exactly like you.
Breathing the same air.
Going through the same phases in life.
Living it until the end.